MW01223366

Inspired to Live an Extraordinary Life

Even through Difficult Circumstances

By

Rebecca M. Pratt

Book cover design: Julie Trisolini

Book cover photo credit: Tim Pratt

ISBN: 9798663537940 (paperback)
Independently published

Dedication

~~~~~~~~~~~~~~~~~~~~~

This book is dedicated to my family and to my dear friends who model their lives after Jesus so beautifully, even while going through difficult circumstances. This book is also dedicated to you, the reader. May you daily be inspired to live an extraordinary life in partnership with our amazing God no matter what challenges come your way.

ACKNOWLEDGMENTS

~~~~~~~~~~~~~~~~~~~~~~~~

I want to thank everyone who had a part to play in these stories, including those who made suggestions for my writing and those who helped in the editing process. Judy Pedersen, Deb Baliko and Jenine Grey, the hours and hours you put into editing this book were such a gift. Others who played a part in this process are Sheryl Mittleider, Laurie Hardie, Kim Koutnik, Mary Rix, Bob Taylor Jr., Ben Odom, and my husband Tim Pratt. Each of you played an important role to make this a great read. Thank you.

COMMENTS ABOUT INSPIRED TO LIVE AN EXTRAORDINARY LIFE

I loved this book! Each person who will take the time to thoughtfully journey through each story, question and prayer in this book will be inspired and equipped for living an extraordinary life. I've been blessed to experience first-hand the beautiful redemptive work God is doing through Rebecca and her team with Orphan Relief and Rescue in both Liberia and Benin. Those experiences along with her writings have worked together to invite me into an "extraordinary life" while also giving me the practical tools to get there.

– Terry Ardizzone, Pastor of Crossroads Moss Bluff,
Lake Charles, LA

You got me walking through these situations as if I was actually seeing them myself with you. Love it, couldn't put it down. A lot of spiritual books give good information but this actually removes the heart of stone and gives birth to a heart of flesh. Thank you, Rebecca!

– Kim Koutnik, Retired – Drug/Alcohol Program
Administrator (City of Tallahassee)
Substance Abuse Monitoring Specialist (Center
for Urban Transportation Research)

Through Rebecca's stories and experiences we have an inside glimpse into how God uses us to unite our community, bring healing, restoration and new life when we serve him fully as a part of a bigger picture, the body of Christ. You will not only be inspired, but hopefully you will answer the heartfelt questions at the end of each chapter and experience God's whisper in your life.

– Laurie Hardie, Co-Host Warm 106.9 FM,
Motivational Speaker, Life Coach and
Author of Did Not See That Coming

In the life of a believer that is walking in obedience, ordinary becomes *extra* ordinary and the natural becomes *super* natural. Rebecca Pratt, through the stories she shares, reveals a loving God who wants all of us to partner with Him to redeem, rescue, and restore.

– Chuck Olmstead, Director of Local Ministry
Development, Salem Media Group, Seattle

Can you imagine living an extraordinary life? It's possible and you will find your inspiration in this book, *Inspired to Live an Extraordinary Life: Even through Difficult*

Circumstances. This spiritual book is a collection of powerful, true short stories from Rebecca's personal experiences with her Orphan Relief & Rescue work in Africa. End of chapter reflective questions, prayer, and songs enhance each message. This book is a sequel to Rebecca's first book, *Inspired to Action*, also a must read.

— *Mary Rix, RN, Ret., Gresham, OR*

This book is for everyone who wants an extraordinary life. Through her mission work with Orphan Relief and Rescue, Rebecca Pratt illustrates how she has heard God in her own difficult circumstances and by fervent prayer she learned that God answered in amazing ways which has led to an ever-deepening trust in Him. With His Book and her prayer, she has leaned on God's guidance, and piece upon piece God built her extraordinary life.

— *Ben Odom, DDS, Ret., Phoenix, AZ*

CONTENTS

~~~~~~~~~~~~~~~~~~~~

*Some names have been changed to protect identities.

Introduction

~~~~~~~~~~~~~~~~~~

I am excited for you to come on this adventurous journey with me through a land of incredible beauty and mystery. You will be introduced to people on the way that you will never forget. Around every corner you will be shown the hidden secrets of a place that few have heard of in the Western world. You will be inspired by our extraordinary and amazing God, who is relentless in His pursuit to redeem each one of us, and all of humanity.

Over the last fourteen years, through an organization called Orphan Relief and Rescue, I have been working with children in Africa who have been abused on every level. I have witnessed what God's transforming love can do, particularly with those whom the world has discarded and forgotten. I have learned that God's business is always to *redeem, rescue*, and *restore,* and that He loves to move mountains to accomplish His purposes.

Orphan Relief and Rescue is an organization my husband and I along with friends of ours, Matt Le Page and Don Clark, founded in 2007. We work to overcome injustice in the areas of abuse, neglect, and trafficking of children in Benin and Liberia, West Africa. This work brings me to Africa on a regular basis as the president of this organization.

In my first book called *Inspired to Action* I take you on my journey and through deep internal struggles as I walked through the process of giving up my life for the sake of all that God was asking of me. In return I got what I never could have dreamed of. I actually found my life and found what I was created to do, and I inspire you to also walk in your own personal journey towards a fulfilling life with Christ.

This second book *Inspired to Live an Extraordinary Life, Even through Difficult Circumstances*, has beautiful stories about how trustworthy God is. As I was writing these stories, not sure what this book would be called, a theme emerged that I could not ignore: God is amazing and extraordinary and as each of us surrenders our life and walks in all that He asks, He turns our ordinary life into an extraordinary life with Him. It is simply what God does. This does not mean our life is without hardship, quite the opposite. Life is hard and many times painful and disappointing. Yet, He always has a good plan for us and others in our path, if we will walk hand in hand with Him. Therefore, I felt the title *Inspired to Live an Extraordinary Life* was very appropriate.

My hope through this book is that you will not see me, but you will see our extraordinary God taking action through the most unlikely people, bestowing His healing touch upon the hearts of the deeply wounded. These stories are His stories.

To set the stage for you, in Benin we work in rural villages three hours north of the main coastal city of Cotonou.

In this area we founded an Orphanage Safe Home for sixty-one orphaned children, and a second safe home for girls who were rescued out of slavery. We have hundreds of children in villages on our School and Feeding Program, children who were intercepted from being trafficked or who were at the highest risk to be trafficked by parents who could not feed them. These same parents are on our Microfinance Program that helps them start a business so they can provide for their families.

In Liberia, our Break the Silence Program empowers children to get help from being sexually or physically abused or trafficked. Our flip chart presentations in schools and orphanages connect children to a hotline we fund, run by the Ministry of Labor's government office. This makes it possible for an abused child to reach out and get help. We also assist many children with their educational costs as they mature and grow out of the orphanages, through our Junior and Senior High School and University Scholarship Program. All this is done through dedicated local staff we have hired within these countries.

To deepen and strengthen your own journey of an extraordinary life, I have included at the end of each chapter, questions for personal reflection, prayers, and songs (available for listening on the internet) specifically selected to enrich this experience.

My prayer is that you will be awakened to all that God created you to be and that every day when you get up in the morning, you will be excited for what God is going to do, in and through your life, no matter what difficulties you may be facing.

The EXTRAORDINARY
Begins with Understanding Who You Are and Whom You Belong To

~~~~~~~~~~~~~~~~~~~~~~~~~~~~~~~~~~

Chapter 1

UNEXPECTED COURAGE

~~~~~~~~~~~~~~~~~~~~~~~~~~~~~~~~~~

"Be strong and of good courage; do not be afraid, nor be dismayed, for the Lord your God is with you wherever you go."
— Joshua 1:9 (NKJV)

Looking into the desperate eyes of a little nine-year-old girl being hunted by those who practice Voodoo, was heart wrenching. If caught, this child would be killed in a ritualistic sacrifice.

I was completely caught off guard and unprepared for this encounter at the end of one of my workdays in Benin, West Africa. Through my work with Orphan Relief and Rescue, on this particular day I had been documenting the children we had rescued from becoming trafficked. It was pouring down rain, past dark, and I was thankful to be finished with my busy day. I was exhausted.

While driving into the Orphanage Safe Home compound, that we founded in 2010 and where I stay when in Benin, I noticed some people ahead of me getting off their motor bikes. I was curious who this could be, as most Benin locals do not like to go out at night on their motor bikes. In this area it is dangerous, because robbers come out after dark. Plus, people never go out in this kind of rain unless they absolutely have to be somewhere.

As we got closer, I recognized one of the men as a trusted social worker and friend, named Alex, whom I have known for years. He used to be the social worker at the local prison in charge of the juvenile department, but now he worked in the main city three hours away. I noticed he was with another man, who was holding a little girl, shielding her from the rain with a black plastic trash bag.

As I got out of my vehicle, Alex greeted me. He apologized for coming at such a late hour, but he said he did not know what else to do. He asked if he could please talk to me. With the rain beating down on us, I quickly told him to come with me under cover, and yes, we could talk. Alex and his friend, who was still holding this young girl in his arms, rushed over with me under a covered entryway. As we sat down, I noticed that this beautiful little girl was physically disabled. She was about three and a half feet tall, yet her legs and arms were severely curved, and she had a huge spinal bulge, preventing her from standing fully upright.

Alex introduced me to this little one, named Rachelle, and to his friend who was her father. He said Rachelle is in great danger and he did not know where else to turn.

He proceeded to tell me her story.

Alex said that people who practice Voodoo and witchcraft believe that they can gain power, wealth, and ironically, protection, with their gods if they sacrifice children with special needs, such as Rachelle. Precious, helpless children in her condition are disappearing. They are being tortured and killed through this brutal practice of child sacrifice.

Rachelle's mother died when she was young, so her father is raising her on his own. He is a mechanic and has to go to work every day so they can eat.

When the police and Social Welfare Office were contacted for help, the father was told that they were overwhelmed with other cases and due to lack of funding and resources, this was not a priority to them. He lives in constant fear for his daughter and does not want to let Rachelle out of his sight. He is terrified of her being kidnapped and murdered by those performing child sacrifices.

He can never leave her at home, so he takes her to work with him every day. Yet now it is the rainy season and the temperature is much colder. He said she has been getting sick, and he fears she won't survive if he has to keep taking her to work with him, where she has to sit in the damp cold all day. He desperately asked if we could please take her into our Orphanage Safe Home to keep her protected.

Oh, my heart ached for this man and his precious child. But I had to explain that not only was our home full and at capacity, but also that we could not accept children who were not true orphans for risk of losing our accreditation.

I asked if a neighbor could watch her while he is at work. He said that is what he did before, but now all the neighbors are scared they will be attacked if someone comes to kidnap Rachelle. He said the people who are doing this are very evil and dangerous. Everyone is afraid of them. For that reason, he was beside himself and didn't know what to do next.

I asked Rachelle if she would sit beside me. She sweetly said yes and came over to me, staring intently into my eyes. As she sat close to me, I wrapped my arms around her little body. I felt how cold her skin was. I quickly tried to think if I had a blanket or anything I could wrap around her, yet I had nothing. So, sadly, all I could offer her was the warmth of my own arms to bring her some comfort.

Listening to their story, I too was at a loss as to what to do. It was a shocking, heart-wrenching situation. I was having a hard time wrapping my mind around the traumatizing circumstances this family was facing.

With their pleading eyes centered on me for the answer as to what they should do next, I literally said, "I have no idea what the solution is for Rachelle, but I know God loves her so much and is trustworthy. Let's pray and ask God to please help us here."

We bowed our heads, and I began to plead for God's mercy and provision for this sweet girl. My prayer went something like this: "Oh, Creator God, I thank you for this precious girl's life. I thank you that you love her so much and that you have a plan for her life. Tonight, we are asking for you to please have mercy on little Rachelle. Please give us some answers as to what to do to help Rachelle and her father. Please protect and provide for this little one. In Jesus' name, Amen."

As I was praying, after each sentence, Rachelle would say, "Amen, Amen." I had to do everything I could to keep tears from flowing down my face. My heart simply could not have melted anymore for this little one. She had my heart!

Here she was, a nine-year-old, listening to adults discuss how people were hunting her and trying to kill her, very aware that God had to come through for her, or she would not survive. This was unfathomable for my Western mind to conceive.

In the Western part of the world, we, as parents or guardians, would be trying to conceal this type of information from our children if we knew they were in danger, for fear they would be terrified day and night. Yet, we clearly were not in America, and in the region where we work, these types of things are what the locals deal with head on. They are very aware that if God does not intervene, they will die or be severely tormented.

While praying, the thought came to mind to hire someone to care for Rachelle. In an area where work is hard to come by, surely someone would want to get paid for caring for this sweet girl.

When our prayer ended, I brought up this idea. Orphan Relief and Rescue could provide the finances if we could find someone to care for Rachelle in the daytime while her father worked. Both men immediately lit up and said, "Yes, if it is someone's job, they surely will take care of her, to ensure they can get paid."

That evening I went to my room and counted out enough money for three months of caretaking and medical necessities for Rachelle, which came to around $200 USD. I shared with her father that we would re-evaluate their situation when I returned in a few months.

To my shock, this all worked beautifully.

One year later, that dear social worker Alex, who has a huge heart for the hurting around him, asked if he could utilize the caretaker money to enroll Rachelle in a private school. She desperately wanted to attend school like every other child her age. Alex assured me that this particular school had good security and that she would be safe there. In light of that, I happily approved this plan, which made Rachelle so excited. She loves going to school!

Now when I see her, she smiles from ear to ear. Each time I visit Benin she and her father can't wait to tell me how she is doing in school.

Rachelle's little life reminds me that we do not have to have the answers to the big problems in front of us, because God is with us, and in us. God is in the business of making a way where there seems to be no way. He will give us the answers as we ask for them. He simply wants us to walk forward, courageously trusting Him.

Working in Benin, the Voodoo capital of the world, still sends shock waves through my mind on a regular basis. With each trip, the stories I hear and am a witness to, seem to be what we would only see or hear about in thriller movies.

Benin is an African nation with incredibly beautiful people whom I love, yet in parts of this country dark secrets seem to loom around every corner. Many of these hidden secrets are quite unbelievable. Children are literally used as sacrifices and are regularly tortured in Voodoo ceremonies connected with that practice.

There are sacrificial altars everywhere, in plain sight, in this particular rural area of Benin. You would not see these altars in the city. They are mainly used for animal sacrifices, yet, as you have just learned, human sacrifice still occurs in secret. Human sacrifice has been illegal for over twenty years, yet secret societies are finding a way to continue this practice.

This is not a place I would have ever imagined I would be working in, yet God divinely set this work in motion. God tends to use the weakest people, so that He can be glorified, and to show His strength through our lives. (2 Corinthians 12:9)

I have realized that I am definitely not a courageous person by nature. I am actually quite the opposite. I love to be comfortable. I am an overly cautious person and do not like to take any chances. To top it off I am also a self-proclaimed germaphobe.

My father told me that as a child I was afraid of everything. He said that whenever we had guests come to the house that I did not know, I would hide under the kitchen table until I felt comfortable with who was sitting in our living room. He said out of all his five kids, he is the most surprised that I am the child that jumps on the plane regularly to go halfway across the world to the parts of Africa where only the brave should go.

I am very aware that I am only able to do this kind of work, living an extraordinary and courageous life, because I have come to know who I am as God's daughter, and I have come to intimately know the God whom I serve. I have trusted Him on numerous occasions, and He has proven Himself faithful over and over again.

In light of my experience, I can confidently tell you that whatever you are going through, that you can also, *"Be strong and of good courage; do not be afraid, nor be dismayed, for the Lord your God is with you wherever you go." Joshua 1:9 (NKJV)*

Question for personal reflection:

- What is something you are fearful about that keeps you from stepping out in faith with what you feel God may be wanting you to take action on?

Prayer:
Heavenly Father, I thank you for creating me and giving me life. I thank you that you are always with me, and you promise to never leave or forsake me. Help me to not walk in fear of the what if's and the unknowns in front of me. Help me to be strong and courageous in all that you ask of me. I choose today to fully trust you with my life and the life of those whom you have entrusted into my care. In Jesus' name I pray, Amen.

Song: "No Longer Slaves," by Jonathan David

Chapter 2

Awakening the Dead

"For this reason it says, 'Awake, sleeper, and arise from the dead, And Christ will shine on you. Therefore, be careful how you walk, not as unwise men but as wise, . . ."
– Ephesians 5:14-15a (NASB)

Albert was a five-year-old child left for dead in his village after his parents had unexpectedly died. Abandoned and alone, he walked around in a death-like state, his hollow-eyed expression a sign of hopelessness and fading life. People in his community considered him a nuisance and daily beat him in order to chase him away. He could not speak, so everyone thought he was deaf. In that location, many children with disabilities are commonly abandoned because it is believed they are cursed if they have any mental or physical imperfections. People are afraid of children such as Albert, and the community did not want to help him. He was living like an animal all alone for months.

The Social Welfare Office notified us of Albert. They said he was barely surviving; yet due to lack of resources they had no place to house him. They pleaded with us on his behalf and told us we were their last hope for this child. If we could not help him, Albert would die.

In our own hometowns if we look closely, we may see others who look as if they are 'sleepwalking' among us. They are the ones who have been abused and hurt emotionally or physically, often to such a degree they cannot adequately process what has happened to them. Unable to endure further pain and suffering, they become numb to life around them and succumb to an emotional coma of sorts. They are simply surviving.

We also see this hollow-eyed look in people in mental hospitals. The emotional pain these people have experienced has left them unable to cope with life. We sometimes see this in people on our city streets. We realize how fragile a human mind can be.

In Africa, particularly in rural villages where we work, we see examples of this all too often. Children who have been used as slaves or have been beaten severely on a regular basis, have this dead-to-life hollow look in their eyes.

The good part about our work is that we have the privilege to help change this 'sleepwalking' state to one of hope. Through love and adequate care, eyes become bright and engaging, and all signs of lifelessness fade away.

For Albert, we were able to put him in a great loving foster home. A doctor concluded that Albert suffered from Ankyloglossia; he was tongue-tied. Once the under part of his tongue was clipped, Albert made quick progress. Within weeks he began to talk, and within a few months he was singing the most beautiful songs. He had no brain damage or hearing loss. He became a fully functioning little boy once properly cared for. I did not recognize him as the same boy three months later. Today he is a completely changed young man, as you can see in the before and after pictures here.

 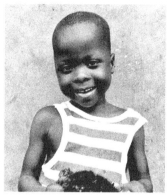

In regard to our own lives, we can ask ourselves questions about our own 'sleepwalking' state. Has our own pain or the pain of our children or other loved ones crippled us emotionally from being able to see anything beyond our own circumstances? Are we struggling with a childhood trauma or abuse that still haunts us? Do we get too busy for anything but work, so that we just barely make it through the day without collapsing? If so, we may need to evaluate how to awaken our own lives from a 'sleepwalking' state.

I often think about Daniel in the Bible, who had overcome incredibly difficult circumstances. Daniel and his three friends, Shadrach, Meshach and Abednego, were stolen from their families at the age of seventeen and were made servants to King Nebuchadnezzar. Their good looks and family status made them attractive additions to the king's household, who put his head eunuch in charge of them. Some scholars say that Daniel and his friends had to be castrated to be in service to the king, as was a custom then for Hebrew slaves. Most young men their age think about their future, of marrying a beautiful woman and having a family. Yet these dreams were stolen from them and shattered.

Despite their circumstances, these four young men never wavered in their faith and love for God. Through the years of service to the king, Daniel's wisdom and honorable actions brought him great favor and he was eventually elevated to be the second man in charge of the entire kingdom.

Daniel had every reason to become crippled and numbed by his circumstances, yet he chose to be engaged and proactive in everything he did. As we can read in the Book of Daniel, he chose to overcome every obstacle thrown at him. Importantly, he kept an active prayer life and stayed close to God. He lived *fully awake* and engaged in life around him, even amidst unbelievable circumstances and personal pain and disappointment.

May we begin to **wake up and be reminded of who we really are and to whom we belong.**

No matter what is going on in our lives, God has a beautiful plan for us. Being fully aware of what we are experiencing in life, He has prepared a plan of health for us through our painful circumstances.

Question for personal reflection:

- What pain in your past may be causing you to be asleep or feel crippled?

Prayer:
Heavenly Father, I thank you for loving me so selflessly and fully. Thank you for pursuing me throughout the day, even when I am not aware of it. I confess that I have been asleep in areas of my life when it comes to my relationship with you. Help me to wake up to who I am in you, and to wake up to all that you have created me for. In Jesus' name I pray, Amen.

Song: "Awake My Soul," by Hillsong Worship

CHAPTER 3

GOD IS TRUSTWORTHY

"The greater your knowledge of the goodness and grace of God in your life, the more likely you are to praise Him in the storm."

— Matt Chandler, Pastor of the Village Church, Flower Mound, Texas

Torrential rain beat loudly on my tin roof and gave me the chance to yell out to God as loud as I wanted. A feeling of hopelessness had hit me and voicing my frustrations to God was all I could do to keep myself from total despair.

Earlier that day I had gone to an internet café to check the status of our Orphan Relief and Rescue bank account. My heart sank when I saw online that we only had two thousand dollars. We had been incredibly frugal with spending, yet donations were at an all-time low.

Within three weeks, I knew we had to wire ten thousand dollars to Liberia and five thousand dollars to Benin, to run our monthly programs, so I began to panic. Was God going to stop providing financially for this work? Were we going to have to close our doors?

Checking our non-profit bank account online is something I do on a regular basis, no matter where I am around the world. Knowing our current account status often determines what we can and cannot do with our programs.

I remember that particular day going back to my room at the Orphanage Safe Home where I was staying, thinking it might be time to start laying off our staff and shutting things down. I remember calling my husband Tim in complete despair and frustration.

When I called Tim, who was visiting Liberia at that time, he seemed unusually calm, and said he would pray, but physically we were quite helpless with both of us being overseas. God had to come through on this one.

After getting off the phone, my anxiety did not subside. I clearly was not sharing the same calmness my husband was experiencing. Feeling in deep despair, I yelled my woes out to God. I let Him know how frustrated I was. My rants went something like this: "Oh God, How I need you right now! I am so frustrated! We are only doing what you have asked us to do. We are living simply, and using every dollar to the fullest, yet here we are, in this desperate state. I am so tired of all of this. I am not going to take on the weight of this work anymore. If you want to close it down, then so be it. I cannot worry about it or take this stress anymore. It is yours!!! Once and for all! I am handing it to you!"

The rest of the day I took time to listen to worship music and just cast my anxieties on Him. It was a complete releasing time. I had come through bouts of anxiety in previous years of doing this work, but this time it was different. It was a releasing to a whole new level.

After many hours passed, I felt compelled by God to go over to the window and look out. As I did, I saw our little boy named Joseph (who lost his parents to AIDS and was HIV positive), just sitting by himself, as all the other kids played around him. He was extra weak that day.

I walked out and put this little one in my arms and nuzzled him as a mother would. He was super stiff and did not seem to want to relax, as he never knows what to do with this kind of love. I just held him close, and he finally gave up his stiffness and relaxed, falling asleep peacefully in my arms.

I thought this was interestingly similar to how I was with the Lord that afternoon. I had been super tense and unable to relax in the supernatural arms of the One that I have known to be trustworthy. I felt in that moment God wanted me to release all of my bottled-up anxiety to Him, and to simply let go and to trust.

As I looked at Joseph sleeping so beautifully and peacefully in my arms, tears streamed down my face. I breathed these words to God, "Oh, how I love this precious little guy, yet I know you love him even more than I do. He is yours. I give him to you. If you want to close this all down, that is your call. I am just going to walk forward in what you ask. I trust you with all this."

As I looked around at all the other children, I began to recall all of their miraculous rescue stories as well. I again breathed out these same words, "They are yours, Lord. They are yours."

In coming home to America, we humbly sent out a letter and email to friends, sharing this immediate need. To our huge surprise, we miraculously had one friend email us back saying that he was sending ten thousand dollars that day to help us.

Soon after, another couple sent another ten thousand dollars, and after that another couple sent five thousand dollars, which got a triple match from their business. To our huge relief, God got us through our lowest giving time during those lean summer months.

The following October our Annual Seattle Gala brought in another generous amount that kept our doors open. Not long after that a small church in Texas let us know that they were closing down their church for various reasons, and anything left in their bank account would be given to Orphan Relief and Rescue. To our shock we received thirty-two thousand dollars from them.

With each donation, I felt as if I were watching a movie. I was a spectator in God's theater. I had a huge sense of gratitude and relief.

All I can say is that God is truly faithful. I am so grateful for those who pray and give as God prompts, and that God uses each of us to make a tangible difference as we choose to say yes and trust Him with the details.

Whatever He wants to do, I trust Him. Even if He did choose to close Orphan Relief and Rescue, *I still trust Him!* All of this is His, not mine. I am just walking in what He asks each day, and that is a beautiful and releasing place to be.

Our finances with this organization are always a daily faith walk, but God continues to show us Who all of this belongs to. Therefore, I can daily lay it at His feet, not my own. Thank goodness, because I do not want to carry that kind of burden. I have finally figured out that this is not my burden to carry.

In my fifty-plus years of life, I have found that God truly knows best. I do not. This work has taught me more about the character of God than I thought possible.

God is waiting for us to let go and to let Him take over every aspect of our lives. Matthew 7:11 reminds us that He is a good father, who will not give us a stone when we ask for bread.

I love the story in 1 Kings 17:9-16. Through a three-year famine, the Prophet Elijah was told by God that a widow would feed him and care for him. Yet this widow was the most unlikely person to care for Elijah because she was dying and was preparing the last bit of her food to share with her only son.

Elijah, knowing the God he served, asked her to please make him a cake first, and that God would not let her flour or oil run out until the Lord sent rain on the land.

By faith she did according to what Elijah asked of her. Once she took action, it says in the sixteenth verse, **"The bin of flour was not used up, nor did the jar of oil run dry,** according to the word of the Lord."

Elijah did not second guess the Lord's provision. It must have been difficult for him to ask a very impoverished woman to provide for him, when she could not even provide for herself and for her son. Yet his faith in the Lord was great, and he knew God's character. He knew God would not abandon this woman and her son in this situation, if she would take this action of faith.

I love that this is the God that we serve.

God proved Himself trustworthy through this story, and He will do the same for you and me.

Today let's choose to trust God with every circumstance of our lives and praise Him through our storms.

Questions for personal reflection:

- What does it look like for you to trust Him with your whole life?
- What is something you need to release fully to God, and entrust to Him?

Prayer:

Dear Heavenly Father, I want to thank you for being trustworthy. I acknowledge that you know what is best for my life, because you created me and know me better than I know myself. I need your presence and help every day. Please help me to trust you with every detail of my life, knowing that you will not give me a stone if I ask for bread as it says in Matthew 7:11. In Jesus' name I pray, Amen.

Song: "The Goodness of God," by Bethel Music

CHAPTER 4

~~~~~~~~~~~~~~~~~~~~~~~~~~~~~~~~~~~~~~

UNDERSTANDING
WHO YOU ARE

~~~~~~~~~~~~~~~~~~~~~~~~~~~~~~~~~~~~~~

"The ultimate measure of a man is not where he stands in moments of comfort and convenience, but where he stands in times of challenge and controversy."
— *Martin Luther King, Jr.*

A young boy around the age of eight was wandering the streets of rural Benin all alone. The stench of urine and dried feces on his body kept anyone from wanting to get too close to him. He was clearly lost and mentally not okay. He also could not speak. As he begged for food with grunts and gestures, people screamed and kicked him away. When police finally picked him up, they assumed he was deaf, since he did not talk and just looked at them blankly when they spoke to him.

Our Benin anti-trafficking team and I had an appointment at the Social Welfare Office the same day this young boy was brought in by the police. Thankfully, the police had been able to give him a shower, but his clothing still smelled of urine when we met him.

The police believed he had been abandoned because they could not find anyone who would claim him as their child. The Social Welfare workers pleaded with us to take him into our care because they had no place to keep him while they continued to trace for his family.

His case was especially difficult because he was also having seizures that would require medical attention. The social workers were in distress over his situation.

I asked to take him outside, away from distractions, to test his hearing and to evaluate him myself. During these simple tests, he just stared at me with no expression on his face. While I was with him outside in the light, I noticed severe scaring on his scalp, an indication of being brutally beaten on a regular basis. He also had a crusty scalp with a severe head fungus that needed to be attended to.

I approached our Country Director, Peter, who is running our Benin Orphan Relief and Rescue programs, with the idea of having him take this boy home temporarily so he and his wife could take him to a doctor for a full medical examination. If they could do this, we could then take the next steps to make sure he was properly cared for. Without hesitating, Peter agreed this was a good idea.

The next day at the doctor's office, it was determined that the child did have some mental disabilities and was very sick with malaria. He was given treatment for malaria, and the doctor shared that his brain most likely had been damaged by severe abuse and/or daily seizures.

After two days of calling him, "the boy," I said, "Peter, we have to give this child a name. We cannot simply keep calling him, "the boy."

Peter quickly responded, "Oh, Rebecca we have already given him a name."

"What did you name him?" I quickly asked.

"We named him Daniel," Peter responded.

"Oh, my goodness, I love that name! It's the name of a powerful and courageous man in the Bible and signifies strength. What a perfect name for this precious boy," I responded.

"Yes, it is," Peter said. "We are believing great things for this child."

Tears began to well up in my eyes as I realized that this nameless and forgotten child had now been given an identity of strength and would be loved and cared for properly by our amazing staff, something Daniel had clearly not experienced until now.

Daniel received anti-seizure medicine and improved significantly. We soon found out that Daniel could hear! When music was played, he would move his body to the beat.

Within the first couple of days of being in the care of a loving family, Daniel was smiling and beginning to show signs of life in his eyes. By week six he had said his first words and had begun to learn to talk. By week eight he was learning how to use the toilet by himself.

The healing and restoration of his mind and body continue to be miraculous. He still is severely mentally challenged, but regularly we are hearing new reports of how well he is doing.

After eighteen months in this loving foster home, he began to remember his given name and where he was from. With countless hours of family tracing, our Country Director and his wife were able to locate his family, that had been looking for him for three years.

Daniel had wandered away from the family, due to his mental state, and was miles away from his hometown. Daniel's mother and father had extensively looked for him with no success. We learned that Daniel's father died in a motorbike accident, two months after Daniel's disappearance, and the mother died not long after that. The family said they continued to look for him but had lost hope with no leads over the years.

They were overjoyed to know he was safe and were eager to get him back when they found out he was alive. The subsequent family reunion was unbelievable and beautiful. Only God could have facilitated such an incredible outcome for this dear boy. Such a miracle!

I am always amazed at what love and proper care can do for these hurting children.

Daniel's story is very symbolic of our own stories. **If we want to live a healthy life with Christ, we have to understand who we are and *whose* we are.** Just as our staff gave Daniel a beautiful name, an identity, this is what the Lord does for each of us.

When we forget who we are or feel beaten down by life from others, God calls us by our name. He tells us that we

are not forgotten. He gives us our identity as His child. We are His son or daughter, a child of the Most High God. We are loved. We are fully accepted. We have been redeemed. We have been forgiven.

When we begin to accept this identity of who we are and who God has made us to be, we can walk through the healing process that God intends for us. Then the power of the Holy Spirit can begin to transform our lives.

For us, coming to a place in our life where we can celebrate the beauty and uniqueness of how we were created, is key to accepting how much God loves us.

Each of us has been made completely different. We have different gifts and talents; we are of different ages, gender, races, and in different seasons of life. One thing we all have in common is that we are incredibly loved and pursued by an amazing Creator who is an extraordinary God.

Through the busyness and trials and pains of life, we can easily forget who we really are and who God has created us to be. We become all things to all people and think about our life last. In this, we lose our identity.

We have to predetermine who we are, not who we think we are, or what life has beaten us down to, but who we really are, so Satan cannot mess with our minds.

Do you feel as if you have lost who you really are at the core, because life's circumstances have beaten you down?

Do you see a beautiful creation God has made, when looking in the mirror?

Do you love this person in the mirror, or are you having a hard time loving that person whom you see reflected back at you?

We cannot walk in our destiny and God's plan for our life unless we come into alignment with our Maker.

Some circumstances in life that can bring us to a place where we forget who we really are, are disappointments with children, spouses, co-workers or friends, and the experiences of divorce, miscarriage, infertility, health crises or job losses. There are many things that can cripple us in life. We can feel as if our legs have been cut off, and we feel immobilized to function normally.

I am here to tell you that what your child or spouse has done, does not define who you are. What you have done in your past, does not define who you are. What health or financial crisis you are facing, does not define who you are. What season of life you are in, does not define who you are.

It is important to remember that **you are a child of God, bought, paid for, redeemed. You are called by name.**

It is also important to embrace the season that God has you in right now. Whatever season you are in, God has woven meaningful experiences into it for you and for those around you. Our attitude through trying times determines everything.

At the same time, when we are discouraged, how can we overcome life's despairing circumstances? For me personally, I have been crippled by many things on that list at one time or another.

**In all of these trials we have to look at how Jesus over-
came the despairing circumstances in His life. Jesus was
desperate for intimacy with the Father, and so we must be
as well. He drew His strength from the Father.**

As we spend time with our Heavenly Father, we will also become refreshed, because His Spirit touches our spirit and con-
firms to us who He is. We are again reminded of who we are.

*…those who wait on the Lord shall renew their strength; They
shall mount up with wings like eagles, They shall run and not be
weary, They shall walk and not faint. Isaiah 40:31 (NKJV).*

God's pursuit and love for us is relentless. He moves
mountains for His children, even when we cannot see it in
the moment.

*So, what do you think? With God on our side like this, how can we
lose? If God didn't hesitate to put everything on the line for us, embrac-
ing our condition and exposing himself to the worst by sending his own
Son, is there anything else he wouldn't gladly and freely do for us?…I'm
absolutely convinced that nothing – nothing living or dead, angelic or
demonic, today or tomorrow, high or low, thinkable or unthinkable –
absolutely nothing can get between us and God's love because of the way
that Jesus our Master has embraced us. Romans 8:35-39 (MSG)*

May your thoughts and thinking align with how God
sees you. If you are having a hard time believing who you
are in Christ, pray the prayer below aloud daily until you
believe the truth about yourself and how God sees you.

Questions for personal reflection:

- Have I forgotten who I really am at my core, due to my circumstances?
- What steps do I need to take to regain my understanding of who I am?

Prayer:
Heavenly Father, I am so thankful for my life and for every breath that you allow me to breathe each day. Thank you for making me special and valuable. Thank you for loving me every day even when I have a hard time seeing it or understanding it. Thank you for redeeming my life with the price of your son Jesus.

Today I am going to choose to walk in who You say I am.
I am not forgotten.
I am Your child.
I am valuable.
I am loved.
I am forgiven.
I am accepted.
I am restored.
I have been created with purpose.
Thank you, Lord, for reminding me of who I am as your child.
In Jesus' name I pray, Amen.

Song: "You Say," by Lauren Daigle

THE **EXTRAORDINARY** HAPPENS WHEN GOD'S PEOPLE TAKE ACTION

CHAPTER 5

WE ARE STRONGER TOGETHER

"Start by doing what is necessary; then do what is possible; and suddenly you are doing the impossible."
                                        – St. Francis of Assisi

"Oh, Rebecca, will you please start another children's safe home in our area?" pleaded the influential judge sitting before me in Benin. "I just arrested a man at the Nigerian border who was trafficking sixteen little children."

"Tell me about this case," I replied. He began to explain that parents in a certain village gave their young children to this man, because they could not feed them. The trafficker told the parents that he would take them to the neighboring country of Nigeria where they could work for their own keep. He convinced the parents that he was helping them, so they would not have the burden of the extra mouths to feed.

In an area where survival is difficult, parents willingly give their children away.

Not thinking anything of the exchange but only of the profit he was about to make, the trafficker then took them to the Nigerian border to sell them into slavery.

The judge said, "Rebecca, these villagers are not bad people; this is just a consequence of poverty. They just want relief from the burden of having to feed their children."

I then asked the question, "Tell me, where did you take the children when you rescued them?"

He put his head down and replied, "That is the worst part of this whole thing, Rebecca. We had nowhere to put these kids, so we took them back to their village. My fear is that they will soon be trafficked again. The parents do not want to keep their children."

"Oh, my," I replied. "That is horrible."

He thanked me for what we were already doing with the Orphanage Safe Home, currently operating at full capacity with sixty-one children, but he pleaded with me to please open another safe home. He daily has children come into the system with no place to go.

As I left his office, my heart and mind were heavy. I breathed a prayer for God to please bring more safe homes into existence or give us and others a game plan for stopping such abuses.

In this particular region, where witchcraft and sorcery are intertwined with every aspect of life, children carry little or no value until they reach adulthood, marry, and have children of their own. If a child becomes orphaned, they believe it is the will of the gods that destined that child to be an orphan, therefore that child carries the lowest value in all of society. In their belief system, since the gods did not have compassion on this child, then they should not as well. An orphaned child frequently becomes the slave in the home of a surviving relative or friend of the parents who died, often leading to the cruel fate of a life of abuse and neglect.

Offering a better way to take care of the orphans would require a major change in their value system. Introducing them to the God who created every life with immeasurable value and worth, is key to transforming their hearts.

For those of us who are personal believers in our Creator God, we know that God had us in mind from the beginning of time. He knew us intimately in our mother's womb as it says in *Psalms 139:13-15 (NIV) For you created my inmost being; you knit me together in my mother's womb. I praise you because I am fearfully and wonderfully made; your works are wonderful, I know that full well. My frame was not hidden from you when I was made in the secret place, when I was woven together in the depths of the earth.*

If you were to guess how much a child is worth on the black market from the streets of Benin, you would probably throw out some large numbers as I did. In my research I was appalled to learn that most children are sold for the equivalent of a US twenty-dollar bill. Sometimes a trafficker will make a deal with a parent desperate for financial help, for the amount equal to one hundred US dollars a year. No detailed questions are asked by the parents as to what will actually happen to the child, as many parents simply do not want to know. To them, it was between giving up their child or watching their child starve.

In a sense they feel they have done themselves and their child a favor. This way of surviving has gone on for hundreds of years in many parts of rural Benin. In these rural villages the average wage is equivalent to twenty-five cents a day. So therefore, if one child is sold with a promise of one hundred dollars a year, the parent feels that this is a good deal.

The last statistics reported for 2009-2017 by the US State Department, show that Benin had forty thousand children trafficked in and through Benin annually.[1] According to our own statistics compiled in 2017 with the parents on our programs, we found that twenty percent of all children in the rural villages where we work were trafficked before we began working there. That is one in five children. These numbers are shocking, as there are only 12 million people in this whole country. Benin has one of the largest child trafficking numbers in Africa with the exception of Nigeria, its neighbor, with the highest trafficking statistics.

After many visits, and hearing story after story from our judge friend in Benin about children being trafficked, an idea came to my mind, which I strongly believe was from God. Why not try putting together a local anti-trafficking team to see what could be done to curb the trafficking numbers in some of these villages?

Putting a team together consisting of trusted locals that were not corrupt and who loved God, seemed like a good place to start. I thought immediately of my translators, who all happened to be pastors. When I presented this plan to them, they were equally excited to be a part of this new mission.

We started in 2013, with a six-month trial in the five largest child trafficking village areas to see how things would go. I asked them not to bring their Bibles into the villages or to tell anyone that they were Christian pastors. I just wanted them to begin by building friendships with those in their path.

Due to the villagers' Voodoo and witchcraft practices, coming in with the message of Jesus was not something that would have been welcomed. Our team members' lives would have been in great danger. We had to come in carefully if we were going to get the information we needed to understand how we could best help the children.

This first six months were incredibly informative and successful. The team learned so much and was able to report regularly about all that was happening in each village. At the end of the six months, our team knew which children were going to be trafficked next and why. They had a list of forty children at the highest risk of being sent away if someone did not intervene.

Our anti-trafficking team found that if we could get these at-risk children into school, the parents would not traffic them. They put the plan together and presented it to the parents. The parents agreed that if we helped get their children into school, they would not sell them.

Eight hundred dollars was all it took for us to get those first forty children their uniforms, backpacks, and school supplies. Tuition, fortunately, was free at the elementary level.

Two weeks after the six-month trial, a co-worker and I were on a plane headed to Benin to document these first forty kids and to formulate a long-term plan for this experiment that, surprisingly, had worked.

A member of our Benin staff picked us up the next morning to take us to these precious children who had been enrolled in a number of village schools. As we drove to the villages, I loved looking out my car window admiring the lovely tropical scenery, thatch-roofed houses and beautiful people.

But once we arrived at the first school, I began to get very emotional. It was a very sobering experience, as I shook each hand and looked each child intently in the eyes, to realize the magnitude of what we had just facilitated. Tears welled up in my eyes as it began to hit me: these children were just saved from a life of slavery and torture. They were no longer just faceless statistics.

We had now demonstrated to these villagers that their lives mattered. **Each beautiful face before me was no longer a stranger. I was given their names, I was told about their dreams, and God was whispering to me about their destiny.**

What was so surprising is how little it took to help these children, whose parents lived in extreme poverty. Unable to send them to school or feed them, the families can so easily resort to trafficking their children. Yet, it only takes thirty-five US dollars per month per child to keep them in school and on our feeding program, which also monitors them so that they will never end up as a trafficking statistic. It is simply unbelievable and shocking to me that children can be saved from such a horrific fate so inexpensively.

A fresh awakening and will to fight came over me after meeting these children. The realization of what we are able to accomplish with God, our staff, and people who give to make these rescue missions a reality, is astounding and humbling. **This is what happens when God's people work together to take action on behalf of those who are suffering.**

After this initial rescue mission, we set up our Microfinance Program. This program conducts weekly business training sessions and awards small loans to parents who want to start a business, with the expectation that they will work to repay the loan within six months. These loans provide the means to choose a better way for parents to provide for their families.

During the first half of the meeting we are able to teach the parents practical aspects of business, such as money management, sales, and customer service. The second half of the meeting is elective, and we share with them about the God of the Universe, who created them unique and special and of utmost worth to Him.

Beautiful things are happening as God breaks down the hard shells of their hearts. Miraculously, we have been able to curb the trafficking in the five large villages where our teams are working. It is no longer acceptable for parents to send their children away, and this whole abusive life cycle is beginning to change before our eyes. As God provides, we plan to take on one village at a time, until trafficking is no longer a common practice in these areas, potentially impacting the futures of thousands of children.

To our shock and amazement, we have been able to intercept over four hundred children from being trafficked and have been able to keep them safe on our food and school program. Over fifty children have also been brought back from a life of slavery. We have been able to help over five hundred parents through our Microfinance Program, who have been able to start businesses and can now feed their own children.

Together we are able to do the impossible. Beninese government workers are telling us that they have never seen such success in curbing trafficking like they have seen with our programs and staff. They keep asking us what our formula is for success.

I tell them that we have an amazing God, amazing staff and amazing people behind us. We are all working together to make the impossible happen.

Just as a body, though one, has many parts, but all its many parts form one body, so it is with Christ. For we were all baptized by one Spirit so as to form one body – whether Jews or Gentiles, slave or free – and we were all given the one Spirit to drink. Even so the body is not made up of one part but of many... But in fact God has placed the parts in the body, every one of them, just as he wanted them to be. 1 Corinthians 12:12-14, 18 (NIV)

This scripture reminds us how we all play different roles as the body of Christ. When we each do our part, remarkable and extraordinary things happen, both domestically and abroad. Location makes no difference to God. When we work together, we are incredibly powerful and strong.

Questions for personal reflection:

- What are you gifted in? Make a list of your gifts, small, medium and large.
- How are you utilizing these gifts for God's kingdom purposes?

Prayer:
Heavenly Father, thank you for the many gifts and talents that you have blessed me with. Help me to always be willing to use my giftings for your purposes. May I daily be aware of what you are wanting to do around me, and to be alert to what you may ask of me. May your kingdom come and your will be done, in and through my life. In Jesus' name I pray, Amen.

Song: "Great Are You Lord," by All Sons and Daughters

CHAPTER 6

TRANSFORMING OUR WORLD

"My little children, let us not love in word or in tongue, but in deed and in truth."
– 1 John 3:18 (NKJV)

.... And what does the Lord require of you? To act justly and to love mercy and to walk humbly with your God.
– Micah 6:8b (NIV)

The first woman who got up to share her testimony at our microfinance meeting shocked me. She said that the only business in their community before we came to help, was selling their children. Upon hearing this, my jaw dropped. Their only business had been selling their children? Was this for real?

One of my favorite things to do when I visit the villages where we serve, is to hear testimonies of parents on our Microfinance Program.

Upon our arrival we are always greeted with singing and dancing. Those on our program are always dressed in bright, beautiful African colors and against a tropical background of palm, banana and coconut trees, the scene looks like a page out of an African storybook.

Yet, the sad secret of this scene is that many of these men and women had trafficked at least one child before we had even met them. The wonderful part is that through God's help and our Orphan Relief and Rescue program, the parents are now thriving and are able to feed their children.

Our Microfinance Program has hundreds of parents who attend our weekly meetings being run by our local staff. They love to share all that God is doing in their lives. Many have committed their hearts to Christ through hearing about a God of love, who has not destined them to a life of poverty, as they had come to accept through their Voodoo and witchcraft religious practices. They are learning about their Creator God who wants them to live a healthy and thriving life. Remarkable life transformations have taken place in front of our eyes; God's spirit is sweeping through this place in miraculous ways.

In the beginning, when our anti-trafficking work was in its experimental phase in the rural villages of Benin, I was regularly shocked by what the parents would tell us about their lives before we came to help them.

Upon hearing that first woman's testimony, that their only business was selling their children, I literally stopped my translator and asked if he had translated correctly. Surely what he had said could not be true.

My translator quickly responded and said, "Yes, I did translate that correctly. This is just what they did in this area, before we showed up to help them." Oh, my heart; I was in shock. I asked the woman to continue her sharing.

She proceeded by saying, "Yet now we do not have to send our children away, because you have shown us a better way. Our new businesses are now this," and she pointed to an array of baskets of consumables that the parents had brought to the meeting to show us, examples of their new thriving businesses. The magnitude of these efforts suddenly hit me.

Then the next woman stood up and said, "I used to feel very ashamed in my village because I could not feed my children. Yet now, my new business is growing, and I am able to feed my kids. I have also accepted Jesus as my Savior. I used to be a very angry woman, as my husband will testify, yet now I am no longer angry. I am happy and kind to people. Jesus has changed my whole life. Today I am able to stand tall and walk through my village like a queen."

One by one the parents shared similar testimonies that brought tears streaming down my face in sheer amazement. This is the God that we get to serve – our God who transforms hearts, lives and circumstances. His restoration is incredible and beautiful.

Fast forward five years. As I walked into one of our regular microfinance meetings, I recognized one of the men present as one of the main traffickers in the area. These meetings take place once a week and are run by our local anti-trafficking staff. I quickly asked one of our Benin staff members, "Is this man a part of our program now?"

Pauline, a trusted staff member, responded with a big, "Oh, yes, he is."

"Oh, my, does this mean he is no longer trafficking children, and did he commit his life to Jesus?" I asked.

"Of course, that is what that means, Rebecca. He has totally changed his life."

"Oh, wow." I said, "I want to hear his testimony, if that is okay."

She quickly responded, "Yes, that would be great!"

I introduced myself to him and asked if he could come over to the side, away from the crowd, to share his testimony with me.

He said he would be glad to share his story but asked why he had to share it in private. He said he would like to share his story with the whole group.

I told him that I was trying to be sensitive, as I felt that he might want to keep some of his story private. At that comment, he quickly responded and said, "I have nothing to be ashamed about. I want everyone to hear my testimony about how Jesus has transformed my life, and how well I am doing in my new business."

I was surprised, but quickly responded for him to please do so, if that is what he wanted to do.

He then got up front, and for the next twenty minutes shared how Jesus was transforming his life, how he used to be a very bad man, but is now a completely different person. He changed his business from trafficking children to selling animals, and he is so happy with his life now.

I was in complete awe of his story. I could not believe what I was witnessing. He is now one of our team's greatest advocates, helping them rescue children from being trafficked, because he knows who is at the greatest risk of being sold next.

God has totally redeemed his story. God is using his experience as a former trafficker to save children instead of harming them.

Early on, we decided as a team, that we would not work to get traffickers jailed, because most traffickers only serve a two-month jail sentence. If we worked to get them put in jail, once their jail time was served, they would return to kill our team. We did not want our team to be in this kind of danger, so we decided that when we encountered these traffickers, we would just try to persuade them to stop harming the children. To our shock, it worked.

We have an incredible Orphan Relief and Rescue staff of Beninese nationals who amaze and humble me with their love for everyone. They pray fervent, persistent prayers and regularly share with us how God is answering them. These are God's people who truly get it. They are showing us how strong the body of Christ is in action.

When we genuinely show Christ's love to others regardless of what they are doing in their lives, or what social strata they come from, or what lifestyle they live, our whole world can change.

Question for personal reflection:

- What burdens your heart for change in your neighborhood, city, country or abroad?
- How might you begin to be open about being part of the solution?

Prayer:
Heavenly Father, I thank you for your kindness and for your gentleness. I thank you for never giving up on me. Help me to represent you well wherever I go and in whatever I do. Help people to always feel your kindness through my life. Please help me to ask for your kingdom to come and your will to be done and give me a strategy as to how you want me to partner with you to accomplish what you want to do. I commit myself to use my life for your glory as you see fit. In Jesus' name I pray, Amen.

Song: "God's Not Done with You," by Tauren Wells

CHAPTER 7

ACTIONS THAT LAST
INTO THE FUTURE

"God never said that the journey would be easy, but He did say that the arrival would be worthwhile."

— Max Lucado

As soon as light shone through little Annie's window each morning, she would quickly get up, get dressed, and rush to the restaurant she had to open each day. She feared getting up late, since she would be beaten severely if she overslept.

At the unbelievably young age of six, it was Annie's job to be the first into the restaurant to get everything ready to open. She was also always the last to leave at midnight, ensuring that every dish was washed and all the floors were scrubbed.

Her parents had given her to an uncle to sell into slavery, so that they might gain income for themselves. He took her to the Nigerian border, where he found two restaurant owners eager to buy her and put her to work in their Nigerian restaurant. For two years she endured unbelievable abuse at the hands of her owners.

Once rescued, Annie shared her tragic story with us. She was not only made to do all their manual labor, but she was also regularly beaten and was never given enough food. She was constantly hungry.

In Benin, we do a lot of family tracing and documentation of children who have been lost in the trafficking world or who have been intercepted before being sold, or who have never been documented as existing. Due to poverty, most families do not have the eight dollars needed for a birth certificate, nor do many parents know how to read or write, so documentation is not a priority. Thus, most of the children we work with rarely know their actual age or the correct spelling of their names. This information is of course needed to enroll them in school, yet gathering all the data is like putting a jigsaw puzzle together. The process always involves finding a parent or living relative, then bringing them to the Social Welfare Office to orally report all the family details, so that the proper information can be put on paper. Finally, we are able to apply for the child's birth certificate through the court system.

When Annie was rescued from her life of slavery, we facilitated her care for four years. First in a foster home, then transferred her to our safe home for girls before we could finally convince one of her parents to come to the Social Welfare Office to begin the oral reporting about her life.

How we got Annie into our program in the first place was quite miraculous. The mother was in our Microfinance Program, and, as part of that program, we inform parents that if they can locate their children, who have been trafficked, and can get them back from where they were sold, Orphan Relief and Rescue will add them to the school and feeding program. This practice removes the financial burden from the family, which is usually why they trafficked their children in the first place. To our shock, Annie's mother had done just that.

Sadly, after living in Nigeria for two years, Annie did not remember how to speak her native language when she finally returned to her family's village in Benin. Annie's parents felt it was hopeless to keep her and tragically, they were preparing to sell her again. They simply wanted to make money off of her. That's when we stepped in. We have been protecting her ever since in our safe home for girls, where she can sleep in peace, eat three meals a day, and go to school.

At the Social Welfare Office, Annie, her father, our Orphan Relief and Rescue Country Director, and I were all present for this oral reporting time.

They started their questions with Annie. "Why are you living with Orphan Relief and Rescue, Annie?"

She responded, "Because my parents sent me to Nigeria to work."

The social worker then asked the father, "Did you receive money for sending her to Nigeria?"

"Yes, I did," he responded matter-of-factly, without emotion.

"How much did you receive in exchange for your daughter?" asked the social worker.

"I received 10,000 CFA" (equal to twenty US dollars), said the father.

"What did you spend it on?" asked the social worker.

"I bought food," he said.

"Is this all you received for her over the course of those two years?" asked the social worker.

"Yes, it was," he responded.

I suddenly realized that I was no longer comfortable being a witness to this conversation, as it had turned into much more than a simple family tracing. It was now a criminal investigation. Our safety would be at risk if this father were to be prosecuted because of his trafficking. Because traffickers rarely serve more than a couple months in jail, we are extremely careful when walking through the family justice questionnaires. For our own safety, we let the courts handle the questions regarding these types of cases.

The questions continued. The social worker turned to Annie and asked, "Were you mistreated in Nigeria, and if so, how?"

"Yes, I was," she responded. "I was beaten many times a day and was hardly given any food. I was always hungry."

The social worker turned to the father. "Did you ever check on your daughter to see if she was being mistreated?"

"No," he responded.

The social worker continued. "If you knew Annie was being harmed, would you have brought her back home?"

"No," he said again.

Oh, my heart! This poor girl was sitting right there, listening to her father's confession about how he basically did not care that she was being hurt, and that he only cared about the money he would receive from selling her. To me, his response went against what a parent's natural instinct should be. Sadly, these stories are all too common in an area where the fight to survive overrules how God created us, which includes loving and protecting our children.

We did not legally need any further documentation from this father, so we gave him money for his transportation home. Then we were able to focus all our attention on Annie.

I said "Annie, I am so sorry you had to listen to your father share what he did. That must have been so hard for you." She shook her head yes.

"Oh, Annie, where your parents have failed you, God has not. God has been with you and will continue to be with you through all of this hardship. One day in the future, you will be going back to your village, and you will be showing your cousins and relatives a better way. You will be the one making sure no other child ever goes through what you have been through." She looked up at me and smiled.

I continued, "Annie, do you believe that is true, that you will be the one to show them how to care for their families and children?"

She shook her head yes again.

I prayed for her heart, and realized a lot more went on that day than the obvious. Although hundreds of children and families have bright futures because of our programs, it is the sweet lives of people like Annie that have the greatest impact and the potential of influencing thousands more. These children know their mission is big, they have extraordinary stories to tell, and they will not be kept silent.

Actions in Liberia that will last far into the future

A young thirteen-year-old girl named Patricia was brought to Orphan Relief and Rescue by the government's Children and Social Protection Office. She was caught stealing in her community and was homeless. It was also known that she had been prostituting herself on the streets to survive.

At that time in 2015, we had the only transition center in all of Liberia. We offered a safe house for children taken out of horrific orphanage situations, but only on a temporary basis until permanent housing could be found for them.

The Children and Social Protection Office would regularly plead with us to take children such as Patricia, who did not fit our criteria for placement, namely being a young orphaned child. With each request, we would evaluate if we could accommodate it or not.

Patricia was one whom we felt we could help for a short time, until a spot in a local safe home for girls opened up.

Her story was one of shock and sadness. After a few months with us, she began to share a bit of her story with our counselor, who was meeting with her regularly. Patricia became more open about her life with me as well. She shared that after her mother died a few years back, her father began to sexually abuse her. She said her uncles also abused her sexually. Her older brother, who did not live with them, was the only man in her family that did not take advantage of her.

I asked her why she did not say no to these men. She said if she refused them, she would be beaten and kicked out of her home, so she stayed with them until she could not handle it any longer, and then she ran away.

What surprised me was that Patricia felt she had no rights, and that she had nowhere to go for help.

Soon after that I had a conversation with another young girl, who came to our Liberian office asking for some school supplies. She said she was tired of having to do sexual favors for her teacher in exchange for simple things such as a pencil and was wondering if we could help her get the supplies she needed.

I began to ask the other young girls in our community in Liberia about this scenario, and I was shocked to learn that this is a common problem for the children living in poverty in Liberia. It is something no one talks about, but every child knows, this is what you have to do to get what you need.

Oh, I could not believe what I was hearing.

We at Orphan Relief and Rescue had just hired a programs director. After processing these stories with him, we both felt we had to figure out how to bring this conversation into the communities. We had to somehow start a public outcry against this injustice, so that things could begin to change. We had to figure out how to empower children in schools and orphanages to know their rights to their bodies, and how to encourage them to get help when being abused.

Our programs director took on this task and created our Break the Silence Program.

We now have a training program in schools and orphanages that teach children about their rights to their bodies and that safety is their right. They are learning that if someone is requiring them to perform sexual acts in exchange for something, this is called abuse. They can say no to abuse and get help.

We have also funded a hotline that children can call to get help, if they are being sexually or physically abused. This year we expect to have this program in hundreds of schools, reaching over 50,000 children all across Liberia.

We have a remarkable staff and great partnerships with other organizations that are training children and other perspective instructors with this new program. It is new to Liberia and is spreading throughout the country like wildfire, which is very exciting on so many levels.

The public outcry has now become a big one, and our staff shares story after story of children who no longer feel like victims. After hearing our Break the Silence teaching in school, some children told our staff that two teachers were making them have sex for grades. Our staff then met with the principal to share this information and those two teachers were immediately fired.

In another story, a young girl informed one of our staff members that her stepfather was raping her every night. Because of the Break the Silence program at school, she realized what he was doing to her was illegal. She never knew she had rights to fight for her protection. She then went home and told her mother what her stepfather was doing to her. Her mother moved her to the safety of her aunt's house. The girl thanked our staff for teaching her about abuse and telling her how to get help. She said she is so relieved now that she is away from her stepfather, because he cannot hurt her anymore.

These actions will last far into the future because God's people are working together. Praying, giving, taking action – when we all work together, we are able to bring freedom to so many. This is what extraordinary living is all about.

Questions for personal reflection:

- What is something in your church or community that you feel you could make a difference in, that you could get involved in?
- Could you commit one or two hours a week to that?

Prayer:

Heavenly Father, I thank you that you are such a huge lover of people and a huge lover of me. I ask that you help me to see things through your eyes. Help me not to be overwhelmed with the many problems in this world. Things that seem impossible – help me to see that anything is possible, through your people coming together to accomplish your perfect will here on earth. Thank you for being my God, my friend, and my lover. In Jesus' name I pray, Amen.

Song: "Rescue," by Lauren Daigle

CHAPTER 8

GOD'S WAYS ARE HIGHER THAN OUR WAYS

"God will meet you where you are, in order to take you where He wants you to go."

— Tony Evans

"For as the heavens are higher than the earth, so are my ways higher than your ways, and my thoughts than your thoughts."

— Isaiah 55:9-11 (KJV)

Holding a starving eight-month-old baby girl weighing only 4.7 pounds was heart wrenching. This little one, named Isabelle, was panting with quick shallow breaths, as if at any minute she would take her last. I honestly did not know what to do, but I sat down and placed my hand on her chest and began to pray. "Oh, God, please help this little girl. If it be your will, spare her life and give this little one comfort and peace." As I prayed, I could visually see and feel her breathing become normal and peaceful. I prolonged my prayer, as I was relieved to be witnessing such beauty in this moment. To my sadness though, once my prayer was over, her panting started up again. Her struggle to take each breath was terrifying. I felt completely helpless. I knew Isabelle would soon die without immediate intervention. She was starving and dehydrated.

My motherly instinct was screaming for me to rush her to the nearest hospital, yet a deep sense in my heart was guiding me to do the very opposite.

This encounter happened in a village in Benin, where we had just begun our anti-trafficking efforts. Just two weeks prior to this visit, we had intercepted our first forty children from becoming trafficked.

After visiting these first rescued children, we were told that their mothers wanted to meet us. We were taken down the road where a large group of women eagerly awaited us.

Upon greeting the women, our anti-trafficking team of four local Beninese pastors, escorted me to the front of the room and said, "Okay, now you must tell these women why they should not traffic their children."

My response was, "Um, right now?"

"Yes, right now," they said.

I had no idea what to say to mothers who willingly give their children away to be servants and end up enduring every unimaginable abuse. Being a mother myself, giving up a child was completely foreign to me.

As I began to thank the mothers for allowing us to help them with their children, the thought came to me about how our Creator God has created mothers to protect their children no matter what the cost. Even most mammals in the wild instinctively protect their young. I posed a question to the women. "What does a mother lion in the wild do if she has babies and someone tries to take them away or wants to harm them?"

One woman responded, "She will kill you."

"Yes," I said, "she will. What will a mama bear do if you come near her babies?"

Another woman chimed in, "She will kill you, too."

"Yes," I said, "that is exactly right. This is how, this same God, has created us women to be with our young. If we do not have this protective instinct in us, then we have to ask ourselves why? Have Voodoo and witchcraft practices numbed us to our natural affection towards our children? Or is there something else?"

The mothers just looked at me blankly. With no life in their eyes, they seemed emotionally dead. In Benin, said to be the birthplace of Voodoo, it seemed to be true, the value of life did not carry much weight.

I had also been informed that some of the women present had sacrificed their first babies to ensure a blessing on their future children, a ritual practice sometimes required by their Voodoo religion. This practice denies the sanctity of life to their firstborn children and robs the mothers of the joys of birthing their first child and numbs them to any attachment to future children. Although this practice is no longer legal, it is no secret that it is still happening in some rural villages. The babies' births are not recorded, so in death, they are never missed by anyone.

As I continued to share from the front of the room, I noticed a small wiggly bundle in the lap of one of the women sitting in the front row. This wiggly bundle was this baby girl, named Isabelle, and she was dying. She was there that day with her grandmother, who watched her during the day but didn't have the means to feed her. I learned that Isabelle's seventeen-year-old mother worked in the fields all day and could only feed her baby once in the morning and once at night. The baby had to wait all day for food.

No one seemed alarmed by this little one's condition. If she died, her death would be considered the will of the gods, and that this was her destiny. In their minds, the child's death would have had nothing to do with a mother who wasn't properly caring for her baby.

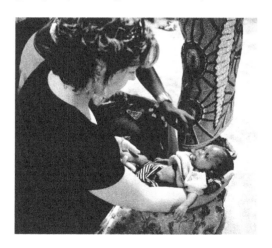

The next day our Benin staff member, Pauline, helped get Isabelle and her mother into the hospital, where, after a four-week stay, Isabelle grew to weigh eight pounds!

Once the mother and baby returned home, every village mother was watching this situation intensely. Pauline involved all the women in the village with little Isabelle's progress. They weighed her weekly in front of the village women. At the same time the mothers were learning how to care for their babies. If a mother was absent, and her baby was suffering from hunger, the nursing mothers were encouraged to share in the nursing responsibilities. This practice, known as "wet nursing," brought immediate results, as the infant death rate began to shrink and continued to do so in the following months.

On each visit to Benin, in the same gathering room where Isabelle once almost died to no one's alarm, these same mothers are now very eager to tell us how thankful they are to have been shown a better way to live and to care for their children.

They now share in the nursing responsibilities when a mother has to work in the fields. They step up to help nurse a baby when they see a neighboring mother unable to feed her own child, and with a sense of pride, they always present Isabelle to me to show me how well she is doing. They push her to the center of the room and say, "Here is your child. We did this!" I love it!

We now see healthy, chubby babies all around. It is a beautiful reminder of what healthy community development looks like when we listen to those whispers in our ear from the Lord, and work in partnership with Him to accomplish His perfect will.

Yes, the Western woman could have whisked this baby off to the hospital and tried to save her life that day. Yet,

God had a much better plan, a plan where all the mothers would learn how to care for their babies, as well as how to work together to ensure that all the babies in their area would not endure the suffering little Isabelle experienced.

If I would have taken Isabelle out that day and taken her to the hospital by myself, from that visit on, every time I showed up, I would have been handed all the sick babies, with hopes I would do the same to save them. That would not have been God's best. He had a better plan to empower this community of women to provide for their own children.

As these women were shown a better way, God was also showing me a better way.

God's ways are truly higher than our ways.

That same day we visited a second village to meet with the mothers there. We had intercepted some of their children from being trafficked as well, and they were also waiting to talk to us. The spiritual dimension of this day, I would not come to understand until later.

Once again, our anti-trafficking team pushed me to the front of a group of mostly women, with a few men, who were eager to hear what I had to say. I just repeated what I had shared with the other group, but this time as I was sharing, it was difficult to get the words out that I wanted to convey. My mind seemed fuzzy and unclear. Struggling for words, I pressed through my speech about how our

Creator God has given mothers a natural instinct to protect their young.

After I finished talking, a woman with hollow looking eyes, rushed up to me, hugged me, and kissed me on the cheek, then ran away. My instant reaction was "Oh, how sweet, she hugged and kissed me." Then a doubt crossed my mind, and I began to evaluate. I thought about how women in this area had never shown affection to me, and that this response was way out of the ordinary. Then it dawned on me; this woman's kiss may have been a curse.

I turned to my co-worker Chase from our stateside office, and said, "Chase, I think I might have been cursed. That hug and kiss was not normal." I am just going to pray nothing attaches to me and that God covers this situation... just in case."

"Yikes!" said Chase. This was his first trip to Benin. "Yes, let's pray this one away."

As the women began to disperse, I noticed two sacrificial altars. I could not see the altars when I was speaking because the women blocked my view, but seeing them now, reminded me that the spirits lingering in this place are alive and active and clearly do not want us there.

That night in my room I got horribly sick. I was sicker than I could remember ever being. I had to go back and forth to the toilet most of the night, which left me weak and barely able to walk.

I kept praying that if this was a curse, that God would break this in Jesus' name, but still I found no relief. I continued to pray against the sickness throughout the night.

The next morning I could barely get out of my bed. I told Chase that he would have to go to the villages without me that day. He and our local anti-trafficking team would have to work on their own to finish documenting the children we had intercepted.

I continued to be extremely sick until late afternoon when one of our Beninese team members came to visit me. I told her that I may have been cursed, even though I prayed against it. I just was not sure what was going on with my body. I was very careful with what I ate and drank, so I knew it was nothing I had consumed.

She recruited the other three Beninese team members, and they had an all-out loud deliverance session in my room. I literally watched them in awe, and thought to myself, I had no idea how to battle in the spirit world like they do. They truly are the right people for this job of working in the territory where they have to fight like warriors to survive the curses they endure on a regular basis. Within a couple hours of their praying in my room, I was completely well.

Now I tell them immediately if I feel I have been cursed. I no longer try to figure it out on my own. I am convinced we are not meant to fight these battles alone. **This is why God has given us each other. We are each other's greatest gift. This is what the body of Christ in action looks like, from the practical rescue mission of Isabelle to the warrior battlefields of the dark side that wants to destroy us**.

For our struggle is not against flesh and blood, but against the rulers, against the authorities, against the powers of this dark

world and against the spiritual forces of evil in the heavenly realms.
Eph.6:12 (NIV)

I can only imagine what must have been going on in the heavenlies on that day. Satan must have known that through our involvement with these women thousands of families were going to come to Jesus; future children were going to be properly fed and taken care of; people would be set free from slavery, abuse, and suffering beyond what we could fathom.

Question for personal reflection:

- What is something you have been struggling to do that you feel God wants you to trust him in, understanding that His ways are higher than your ways?

Prayer:
Dear Heavenly Father, I thank you that you are the most powerful God of the Universe. I thank you that your ways are always higher than my ways. Help me to fully trust you when you prompt my heart to take action or to not take action. Help me to not walk in fear, but in trust daily in your guidance, protection and direction. I love you for who you are in my life. In Jesus' name I pray, Amen.

Song: "Reckless Love," by Bethel Music

CHAPTER 9

AN UNEXPECTED GIFT

*"Wherever people love each other and are true to each other
and take risks for each other, God is with them, and for
them and they are doing God's will."*

– Frederick Buechner

L ooking back over my early life experiences, I can
see they were the beginning of my awareness of how
God works through His people. One does not have to be
in Africa to realize this important truth about the body
of Christ in action. For me it began in Texas.

Moving to Texas in 1984 when I was fifteen years old was
not something I was excited about. My older sister Debby
was preparing to attend Christ for the Nations, a Bible
college in Dallas, Texas, and my dad was feeling drawn to
move us as a family down south. After living in Washington
for eight years, this was not happy news to me. I had a boyfriend and lots of good friends that I did not want to leave
behind. My father gave us six months to prepare ourselves
for the big move.

As the time grew closer to our departure date, my mom felt she needed more time to prepare herself and the household to move. Since it was August, my dad decided that he would take the three older siblings to Texas to get us started in school. He would also at that time find a job. Then he would return to Washington and move my mother and younger two siblings to Texas.

Saying our goodbyes was not easy, but we had been talking about this for six months, so we were actually relieved to finally get on the road to see where this new adventure would take us. My boyfriend and I had broken up by then, so my heart was no longer in turmoil over the impending separation from him.

Driving into Texas in August was a shock to my system, as the humid 105-degree weather took my breath away. Living in Washington, people came alive in the summer months, and I was outside every waking moment to enjoy the 80-degree days. Yet in Texas, summer was hibernation time, going from one air-conditioned place to another just to avoid the heat. Texas was going to take some getting used to.

Upon arrival in Dallas, my dad was on a fast track to get us settled. First, my sister Debby was dropped off at her dorm room at the Bible college, and then my dad found us a nice rental home in Fort Worth, a forty-five-minute drive from Dallas. He enrolled my brother Bobby and me at the local high school. He then secured a job for himself and bought an inexpensive car for Bobby to drive while he was away.

While doing all these things, my dad's top priority was to find us a great church to attend. He was very vocal about making sure we would have a healthy support group around us who loved God.

We were excited to find a great church, not too far from our new home, with a huge youth group. After all these things were established, my dad returned to Washington to move our mother and other two siblings, Daniel and Rachel.

My brother Bobby and I had no furniture, but we were not complaining, because we knew Dad was coming back soon to furnish our home. We became popular among our friends in the neighborhood, because we had no parents, no furniture, and apparently no parental rules either.

We went to school every day, and after school Bobby would go to his new job. We quickly fell in love with our new church, and weekends were full of fun youth group activities. Texas was turning out to be a great place to live for my brother and me because of all our amazing new friendships.

Two weeks after my dad arrived back in Washington, my father called to let us know that the move was costing a lot more money than he had expected. He was going to have to work a few weeks longer in Washington to get the money needed to move all our belongings. He said he felt horrible about leaving us down there by ourselves but did not know what else to do.

At that time, Bobby and I were not too concerned, as we were having a ball with our new friends. Parents loved us in the neighborhood because we were not the alcohol partying type. They felt we were safe for their kids to hang out with, so our home never lacked visitors.

To get our exercise in the evenings, Bobby and I would regularly run a couple miles around our neighborhood, which soon turned into somewhat of a neighborhood running club, with five or six of us teenagers running together. After living on a small island in Washington for eight years, with no neighbors with kids our ages, this was the kind of life we had always dreamed of.

One neighbor friend Ockie, who was sixteen and worked at McDonald's, would bring us left-over food after his evening shift. He said he felt sorry for us not having parents who would cook for us every night. He was our hilarious African American friend whom we had tons of fun with. He always spoke his mind quite vocally about how he felt about every detail of our lives. He would look around our big empty house and say with his strong southern accent, "Y'all, are you sure your parents are coming back to take care of you?" He was the only child at home with a single mother who doted on him, so this whole situation was very perplexing to him.

After a little over two months of a fun-filled life, things started to fall apart. Our vehicle needed repairs and most of Bobby's paychecks were spent on keeping it running. Not much money was left for the other things we needed. Dad tried his best to help us, but he was feeling overwhelmed with the extra expenses as well. The final straw was when the muffler system broke down and the car became impossible to drive. The cost to repair it was way beyond what we could do at that time.

Dirk, our dear friend from church, who was nineteen at the time, loaned us one of his vehicles, which was a huge answer to prayer. Sadly, within a couple of weeks of driving that car, Bobby got in an accident and totaled it.

We were both uncertain as to what to do. We felt alone and hopeless. My poor father and mother were beside themselves as well, as their circumstances in Washington were not going as planned. They, too, felt helpless.

Bobby and I were praying intently for God to help us, as we needed a true miracle of God's intervention. We were not sure how we could live on our own without a vehicle.

The accident happened on a Saturday, and the following day on Sunday, our friend Dirk came to pick us up to go to church. We had wrecked his car, yet he continued to be there as much as he could for us. He never made Bobby feel bad about the situation. He genuinely just showed us unconditional love.

Both Bobby and I were in deep turmoil at church that Sunday. During the worship/singing time, the worship leaders asked if anyone needed prayer, they could come to the front where people would pray for them. I immediately got up and went forward. I went straight up to a couple that looked friendly and spilled my heart out. I am sure this poor husband and wife praying for me did not know what just hit them.

After the service, this same couple came up to Bobby and me to get more details about what I had told them. After sharing more about our situation, they asked us to consider living with them. They said they had a son and daughter our same ages and Bobby could drive their extra vehicle as long as he needed. They asked us to talk it over with our parents on the phone, and if they agreed, we could move in with them that day. They would like to take care of us and have us be a part of their family until our parents returned.

This was the most wonderful thing to hear. We were going to be taken care of! Oh, how amazing that sounded!

Of course, our parents were relieved and grateful. That evening we moved into this wonderful family's home and became a part of their lives. They even asked my brother to give up his job, so that he could focus on his schooling, which he subsequently did. They would provide financially for whatever we needed while we were with them.

We ended up staying with this family until our parents arrived about a month later. This couple was amazing to us, and their kids became our good friends. They were a gift from God on every level.

One of the remarkable things about this story is that for my brother Bobby and me, God used this entire experience to grow our faith and to strengthen us. What many people would consider to be tragic, ended up being something that God used to make his love and care real to us in life changing ways.

My father would later tell us that for him the experience had been terrible, and that God used this time to get to the root of some of his wrong attitudes and thinking. What my dad considered to be a season of discipline for him, the Lord used to show His amazing power and care for us on very personal levels at our young tender ages.

I also learned what being a part of a healthy church family is supposed to be like. I learned that humbling myself and asking for help when in distress is an important part of healthy living. I learned that allowing people to help me and to show me unconditional love is what God uses in my life to strengthen me when I feel at my weakest points. Once I am strengthened, I then, in return, am able to be the giver and helper to those in need around me. It is this beautiful cycle of life that God has taught me throughout my life.

No matter where I have lived or traveled, I always look for a healthy church body to be a part of. It is a lifeline that God has given us to utilize no matter where we are.

And let us consider how we may spur one another on toward love and good deeds, not giving up meeting together, as some are in the habit of doing, but encouraging one another – and all the more as you see the Day approaching. Hebrews 10:24-25 (NIV)

Our church body has been crucial in helping us as a family walk through difficulties and life's challenges. It has been a place to serve and to be served. We are incredibly blessed when we can be a blessing to others, and when we experience hardships ourselves, we have a beautiful family ready to pray and to rally around us.

In our work in Africa, we link arms with thriving churches, so that we can watch God in action through amazing people who demonstrate the love of Jesus to those in their path. Our foster parents who care for the children in our programs in Africa come from these healthy non-corrupt churches. Many of our Orphan Relief and Rescue staff come from these churches as well. We have learned what the body of Christ looks like worldwide, and it is beautiful. Yes, there are many corrupt and not-so-good churches out there, but if you seek out the good ones, you will find them.

More valuable lessons in our neighborhood

Knocking on the door of an elderly woman who was in distress, yet not being able to get into her home to help her, was very frustrating.

After church in 2017, a few friends of this woman, named Pat, shared with me that they had not heard from her in over a week and were worried that something might be wrong. Knowing I lived close to Pat's apartment, they pleaded with me to please check in on her.

When church was over, I went straight to Pat's home and knocked on her door over and over with no response. I then called her name numerous times from the door. I could faintly hear Pat yelling back at me that she could not come to the door. I then called her phone and yelled from outside for her to answer it. She again faintly yelled in response, that she could not reach her phone to answer it.

I called our pastor and some other church friends who knew Pat well, to see if anyone knew how I could get in, but no one could help me. Their suggestions were to call Pat's son, who lived an hour away, or to just call 911. I got no response from Pat's son. Before calling 911, I tried to get Pat to tell me if there was a key hidden anywhere.

To my relief through our yelling back and forth, I did get Pat to tell me where a hidden key was located outside on her patio. Once in her apartment, I found her in a recliner very pale and unable to get up, sitting in a pool of urine. She seemed delirious and was not making sense when she talked. I finally was able to understand her enough to realize she had not been able to get out of her chair for days. She had nothing to drink or eat and had not gone to the bathroom in all that time. I quickly got her water to drink and called 911 as she clearly needed medical help.

When paramedics got there, they said she may have suffered from mini-strokes, and her vital signs all pointed to severe dehydration. They felt they should take her to the hospital for treatment. Upon hearing that, she quickly got her spunk back and refused to go to the hospital, claiming she was fine. We pleaded with her to go, but with no success. The paramedics said they could not take her against her will, even if they felt she needed to be hospitalized.

In my frustration with Pat not heeding this medical attention, I recruited their help to get her to the bathroom, so I could get her cleaned up. The paramedics left soon after that. Pat insisted she just had the flu and that she would be okay. After helping her in the bathroom, I got her food and more water and then cleaned up her chair.

Her bed sheets were also deeply soiled. I quickly began to strip the bed to wash the sheets, but Pat yelled at me from her kitchen table to stop when she saw what I was doing. She said she did not want me cleaning her sheets.

I replied back to her, "Who is going to do this then?"

She said, "I will. Just please leave them alone."

Knowing her son rarely visited her and that she had no one else to help her, I told her, "I love you and this is what love does. If you refuse to let me help you then you are refusing my love."

She hemmed and hawed and made some comments that were not very nice, as I lovingly did what needed to be done to make sure she would be okay.

For the next week I went over twice a day to bring her food, to change her wet bedding, and to do her soiled laundry. With each day, she had greater clarity of mind and her speech grew more understandable.

She began to soften her heart towards me, as I would change her bedding and help her into a fresh and clean nightgown. I would daily remind her that she was loved and was worth all this love and effort.

I let our pastor know that I was leaving for one of my African trips soon, so she immediately enlisted the help of some women to take over the routine. Pat refused most professional help, and her only son decided that he was not going to make his mother do anything she did not want to do. For that season, these church women were the ones who kept Pat alive.

I had many personal conversations with Pat, who was in her late eighties, about why she was refusing professional help. I first thought that maybe it was due to a lack of finances, since she had rented the same two-bedroom apartment for thirty years with no upgrades. She lived like a woman in poverty. To my great surprise she shared that she was very well off financially. Yet even with her wealth, she had no desire to take care of herself with that money.

Pat had been a nurse for forty plus years. She had always taken care of everyone around her and was used to being in charge. She was also a widow and had run her own life for many years, never having to depend on anyone. She had become very independent and self-sufficient.

I tried to evaluate why she refused to help herself with her resources and why she made it so hard for me to help her when I first discovered her. Was this a show of power, of her not wanting to relinquish control of her life? Was she just not feeling worthy of people's love? Or maybe a little of both? One thing was certain, she was an incredibly stubborn woman, and nobody was going to tell her what to do.

The beauty in all of this was watching the body of Christ in action. The church women rallied together to drop off meals, to sit with her to make sure she ate, and to take her to her medical appointments. Her son never did step up to help her, but the church body did. I was so proud to call each of these women friends. The church body saved her life, both physically and emotionally. They were instrumental in showing her how loved she was and how important her life was.

In looking back at this situation, I thought how symbolic this story is for our own lives. How many of us are sitting in our filth, like Pat, crippled by life's circumstances? Maybe we are afraid to fully trust that God has the best for us, or maybe we do not feel fully worthy of God's love for us, and therefore sabotage ourselves through addictive behaviors. Yet, Christ has given us everything we need to be healthy and whole and to walk in freedom, if we will simply ask Him to help us, and be willing to give Him control of every area of our life.

Pat had plenty of money to get her all the professional help she would ever need. If she wanted, she could have chosen to live in a retirement home with 24/7 care, yet she was choosing to live in her painful circumstances. Had it not been for the numerous caring people pushing themselves into the situation, she would have died in a urinated mess.

Like Pat's *physical* bank account, our *spiritual* bank account is also bursting at the seams with blessing and favor that God has in store for us. We just have to choose to accept His free gifts and walk in them daily. Jesus has paid the ultimate price for our every sin, past and present. We have been adopted, forgiven, loved, and given the power of the Holy Spirit to guide and lead us. We have been given a personal relationship with our loving Father God who is so for us. We cannot live as if we have no resources any longer. We cannot wallow in our past, our hurts, our pain or bitterness. God has shown us a better way and a beautiful way to live. But some of us, like Pat, are having a hard time utilizing our hefty bank account.

I am here to tell you to pick yourself up and choose to accept all that God has for your life. Allow yourself to be deeply loved by God and by others. God says you are worth it.

Questions for personal reflection:

- What is something you need a healthy church body to rally around you for?

- What will it take for you to be willing to share this with your church or a mature friend who loves God?

Prayer:
Dear Heavenly Father, I thank you that you are always working to bring help and healing to my life. I thank you for the healthy friendships you have given me. Help me to never fear being open with a few close friends who love you, especially when I am in need of prayer, accountability, or moral support. Help me to live honestly and lovingly when I see those in need around me as well. In Jesus' name I pray, Amen.

Song: "I Am Not Alone," by Kari Jobe

THE **EXTRAORDINARY**
CONTINUES WHEN WE UTILIZE
OUR SPIRITUAL GIFTS

CHAPTER 10

EXTRAORDINARY LIVING THROUGH THE HOLY SPIRIT

"The best and most beautiful things in this world cannot be seen or even heard, but must be felt with the heart."
— *Helen Keller*

Josephine, an eight-year-old girl, was peacefully sleeping in her bed at home, when she was abruptly awakened in the night. Terrible sounds of her mother and father screaming in another room made her jump out of her bed. She, along with her younger siblings, ran to where the screams were coming from. Little did they know that this night would be the most traumatizing night of their lives, as they stumbled into the scene of men running, with machete's in hand, who had just attacked and killed their parents.

They watched these men run away with the money box that Josephine's father had freshly filled that day at the bank to pay his employees for the week. This had been a burglary that went very wrong. Miraculously, the men quickly left without harming the three children.

Police would later explain that when they arrived on the scene, they witnessed the most gruesome sight they had ever experienced. Trying to console children who were crying hysterically, completely in shock and horror, was something no training could have adequately prepared them for.

The Social Welfare Office brought the three children to one of our safe homes that would offer them shelter and the utmost protection. The next few years for these children were painful, as we watched them struggle with the tragic loss of their parents.

The little two-year-old sister cried each day for about six months. She could not be left in a bed alone at nap time or bedtime without her screaming. She pretty much lived on a sibling's back throughout the day (as they do in Africa) and in a caretaker's bed at night.

Josephine and her brother did not want to talk about what had happened; they just wanted to be like all the other children around them, yet the sadness in their eyes spoke volumes.

With each visit I would focus on these three children to evaluate how they were doing. To my surprise, little by little, they seemed to be recovering.

Daily corporate prayer times with all the children and constant encouragement for them to pursue their own relationship with Jesus were keys to this recovery. As they began to see themselves through the eyes of Jesus, the sadness in their own eyes began to fade. They began to realize that they were loved, valued, and not forgotten in this world full of hurt and pain.

Fast forward four years. I had heard that Josephine was still having nightmares at night. I made it a point to have some time to talk to her about this, so on one of my visits I took Josephine by the hand and brought her to meet my friend and trusted female translator.

I asked Josephine how she was managing to recover from the traumatic loss of her parents. She shared about the nightmares, that when she goes to sleep, she is awakened by the memory of the screams of her parents, and then the images of that night play over and over in her head. She does not know how to escape from these nightmares.

As she was standing in front of me with tears in her eyes sharing from her heart, I suddenly heard a gentle whisper in my mind speaking to me these words: If this were your biological daughter, and you had been the one murdered in front of her, and a woman was trying to tell her it was going to be okay, what would you want that woman to say to your precious girl? Oh, my, this question really made me think and made my answer so personal. I instantly wanted this girl to have a beautiful message of love from her mother and ultimately from Jesus.

I asked Josephine if I could hug her and she quickly responded yes. I wrapped my arms around her and told her how much her mother loves her and will love her into all of eternity. I told her how sorry her mother was that she could not be here in person for her. I shared how proud her mother is of her as a daughter and as a young lady, that she is so proud of how she takes care of her brother and sister and of how strong she has been. Tears dripped down my face, as I envisioned myself as Josephine's deceased mother who was given this rare opportunity to share with her beloved daughter how much she loved her. I had no idea this would become an incredibly emotional moment in time, that God's heart was pouring down through my words and actions into this hurting girl's life. I tried hard not to break into an all-out sob fest. Thankfully Josephine could not see my face, as her head was resting on my chest and she was completely oblivious to my tears.

My translator was telling me in English to stop crying immediately, as she herself was becoming an emotional mess. Her tears were equal to mine.

What was beautiful about this whole moment was that Josephine was simply just basking in all of my loving words, completely unaware of my translator and me. I continued to speak words of love to her, being very careful to control my voice and not choke up. The last thing I wanted to do was ruin this special moment by making it a sad time instead of one of beauty and healing.

Once I regained my composure, I had her stand directly in front of me. I looked deeply into her eyes and said, "Josephine, from here on out, when you have a nightmare, I want you to envision Jesus and your mother rocking and holding you like we just did here, telling you how much you are loved. Can you do that, Josephine? Even though your mother cannot be with you, Jesus is always going to be with you and will never leave you. He is your protector, your father, and best friend."

She responded with an "Okay," then hugged me, and went on her way. Through the rest of the week that I was there, when I was near her, she was my little shadow, always by my side.

A few months later when I returned for a visit, I asked her how she was doing, and if the nightmares were still there.

She said, "I am doing good, and no, the nightmares are no longer there."

I said, "Oh my goodness, that is amazing. How did that happen?"

She quickly responded, "I just do exactly what you told me to do and it works."

Okay, I have to confess, I was sure hoping that what I had said to her would work, but in my heart, I really had had my doubts. But I have learned through this experience and many others like it, that **the mystery and the wonderment of our God is way beyond what we can fathom or imagine. Through His Spirit He comes in with a sweep of His healing and soothing touch, that only He can bring.** I do not understand it, but I see it every day. He truly is the Master Healer.

This picture is of my granddaughter looking up in awe and wonder at Christmas lights. It is a perfect illustration of how we all should feel when it comes to what God is doing all around us.

God's spirit is living inside of us and helps us in our weakness. This is where our power comes from to do all that God asks. He truly gives us everything we need when we need it.

In the same way, the Spirit helps us in our weakness. We do not know what we ought to pray for, but the Spirit himself intercedes for us through wordless groans. And he who searches our hearts knows the mind of the Spirit, because the Spirit intercedes for God's people in accordance with the will of God. And we know that in all things God works for the good of those who love him, who have been called according to his purpose. Romans 8:26-28 (NIV)

But you will receive power when the Holy Spirit comes on you; and you will be my witnesses in Jerusalem, and in all Judea and Samaria, and to the ends of the earth." Acts 1:8 (NIV)

We are meant to live a radical, supernatural life in partnership with Christ no matter where we live.

Most of my African friends believe everything is spiritual, that there is nothing not connected to the spiritual world. They take the spiritual realm very seriously. As Christians in Africa they regularly fast and pray all night and expect to see many breakthroughs.

In the Voodoo religion people are either complacent, thinking things are the will of the gods and there is nothing they can do to change their lives, or they get radical and try to appease their gods or gain power from them in the unseen spirit world by making sacrifices.

In the Western part of the world we separate the spiritual from the physical. If we cannot touch it, feel it, or see it, we have a hard time believing it. I personally have come to believe that everything we do does have a spiritual component and consequence to it. **I have learned that the practical physical actions we take in life bring about a supernatural reaction that God facilitates through His Spirit, at His will through our obedience. When we say yes to what God is asking of us, we help bring into existence what God wants to accomplish here on earth, bringing a part of heaven to earth. Through the words we speak and the actions we take each day, we can produce either life or death in our lives and in the lives of others.**

God is daily weaving and spinning to restore and heal people's lives. He wants us to walk in the supernatural power of His Spirit that He has given us each day to see people set free, not in a weird way, but in a very natural way through our everyday lives in service to Him.

When we step out in faith and watch God do beautiful things in front of us, such as with Josephine, we begin to fall more in love with Jesus. We also begin to grasp the kindness of the Lord and His steadfast love that never ceases.

The steadfast love of the Lord never ceases; his mercies never come to an end; they are new every morning; great is your faithfulness. Lamentations 3:22-23 (ESV)

Question for personal reflection:

- What is something that needs a part of heaven brought to earth, through your life?

Prayer:
Thank you, Heavenly Father, for your Holy Spirit in my life. I thank you that I do not have to figure out what to pray or what action to take, because you will guide and direct me through your Spirit. Help me to trust your Spirit more and to realize I do not always have to figure out the answers, but need only to ask you to guide and direct me and to show me what to do. Help me to listen to your promptings of your Spirit in my life. I commit to be a better listener. In Jesus' name I pray, Amen.

Song: "Here as in Heaven," by Elevation Music

CHAPTER 11

EXTRAORDINARY LIVING THROUGH PRAYER

"Our public worth is determined by our private time with God."

— Oswald Chambers

"If my people, who are called by my name, will humble themselves and pray and seek my face and turn from their wicked ways, then I will hear from heaven, and I will forgive their sin and will heal their land."

— 2 Chronicles 7:14 (NIV)

Women in prison with their babies is not something we are used to seeing in the Western part of the world. Yet in Benin they allow the pregnant women in prison to deliver their babies there and to keep them until the age of five. They have separate quarters from the other prisoners.

In giving out clothes to the children at the Orphanage Safe Home we founded, I had little dresses left over that had been given to me by a women's sewing group on Whidbey Island in Washington. Knowing the children in prison were in need, we decided to take the rest of the dresses to them.

It turned out that my translator/pastor was scheduled to preach in the prison just a few days later on Sunday, so my co-worker Don Clark and I decided that this would be a perfect time to deliver the dresses. We would then buy a few shirts in the market for the little boys.

The local pastor suggested that Don speak at the prison service to give people a taste of the Western man's sermon. Don was excited about this because he volunteers in the prisons in Texas and has a real heart for the people who are incarcerated.

Walking into the prison was a bit shocking to me. There were 900 prisoners in an area that we were told should have only held 100 prisoners. Once we came into the compound where the men were held, all the men were out in the open. There were no individual cells. We had to walk through the crowd of rough-looking men to get to the location where the church service was to be held. As the only woman in this group, I was very uncomfortable with this whole situation. I had to fight my internal fears and just walk forward, staying close to Don and my translator.

The service went great, and the men were deeply touched by Don's message. They felt valued by us foreigners, who would take the time to come share with them in their distress.

After the service, we prayed for some of the men, then went to see the mothers and babies in a different section of the prison. We were escorted in by a social worker. When we walked in, the women just looked at us with blank stares. They were clearly wondering what we were doing there. I was also curious about them. I did not want to just say hello to these women with babies attached to their hips; I wanted to know more about their lives and stories.

We gathered them around us, and I asked my translator if he felt it would be okay for us to pray for these women. He said yes, that would be a good idea. We asked the women if they would like to share their stories with us or have us pray for them, that we would love to do that for them.

To our surprise they immediately lined up to pray with us. The first woman shyly came forward. She kneeled down and told us her story. She said she had been in prison for two years because her village thought she had sold her first baby to be killed for a Voodoo sacrifice. She was in prison for murder. She told us her baby had been sickly from the time he was born. After a year and a half of doctor's visits, she went to Nigeria to do business with her uncle for a few months to earn money to pay for the medical bills. Her baby died there. When she returned home without her baby, the villagers accused her of murder.

After the trial, the judge found her innocent. Yet two years later she was still there and during this time she had given birth to her second baby, who was now twenty months old.

The next two women came forward together very shyly. The first one began to speak and said that one of her five children had become mentally ill, so she took him to the village doctor (a witch doctor) to try to cure him. The village doctor diagnosed him as having a curse put on him by his own mother, her best friend, and the best friend's mother. So, all three women were thrown into prison because putting a curse of harm on people is illegal in Benin.

Two of the women were pregnant when they arrived and delivered their babies in prison. Also, they each had left four children behind at home in their village. After one month in prison the judge ruled all three women to be innocent and said they would be released within the month. But eight months later they were still there.

One woman after the next shared her tragic story. Each story was complicated, and the judge had delayed decisions on their cases.

But, for the women who had already been proven innocent, I felt I could not stand by and do nothing. Just a simple visit to the judge to ask him why these innocent women remained in prison could not hurt, right?

That next day was a Monday. I had no idea if the judge would even see us, but we headed to the courthouse first thing that morning with the women's case histories in hand. To our surprise, after only thirty minutes of waiting in the hall with other locals, we were escorted into the judge's office.

The judge let us know that on a normal day his hall would be completely full of cases, and there would be no way he could see us without an appointment, yet this week was different. He was without a secretary, so he could not close any cases. He was awaiting a new secretary from the main courthouse in Cotonou (Benin's largest city and the seat of government). So, he said, "You have my full attention today. What can I do for you?"

I first affirmed him in what he was doing for his people, working for the justice of his nation. I handed him my Orphan Relief and Rescue business card and said we were both working for the same thing, justice, yet my focus work is with children. I shared what we had heard in the prison and pleaded with him, very kindly, to please release the innocent women so they could return to their children who needed them at home.

He said he was aware of the cases, and yes, the women were innocent. He committed to make their cases a top priority and assured me he would release the women as soon as his new secretary arrived. (We were told there is no rhyme or reason for when a case is heard or decided. If someone isn't advocating for a person in prison, that person can stay there for years, innocent or not.)

The judge asked more questions about what we were doing in Benin. He became very friendly and said that he would like to help us if we ever needed him for anything. He encouraged us to please continue to help his country. We thanked him for his time and left his office, knowing we had acquired a new friend.

As we walked out of the office, my translator whispered to me, "Oh, Rebecca, you could have freed many more innocent people today, because that judge was willing to hear whatever you had to say. You had his full attention. Please, can we go back to the prison right now and get more stories and names of the many more innocent people who need to be freed? If you were to stay even a couple weeks longer in Benin, we can free so many more people, Rebecca."

As incredibly tempting as this sounded, I felt a deep cautiousness in my spirit to not react. I felt an overwhelming peace that today we were done with the task that God had set before us. At the same time, I knew I needed to spend some quiet time with God to make sure I did not do anything outside of what God was asking, because the temptation was great to try and rescue more innocent people. Yet at the same time, I did not want to touch anything that God was not mandating us to do. I did not want to walk in my own understanding with this one. God had to be the one directing our every step.

Upon arriving back to my guest room at the Orphanage Safe Home, I loved on the kids for a bit, then went into my room to be alone. I needed some time with God to determine if I had done the right thing by not going back to the prison to try to get more names of innocent people.

As I quieted my heart and mind before God, I had a deep sense that God was saying "Well done." Then a new thought came to mind. The women in the church that donated the little dresses were the ones who began this entire chain of events. **Through their acts of kindness four innocent women were going to be set free from prison. It started with these women and it needed to end with them.** They were the ones who needed to be tasked with praying these women out of prison and to pray for the broken and dysfunctional judicial system. God wanted to do something bigger. He did not just want to free four innocent women; he wanted the whole judicial system transformed. This could only be done through prayer, and this church was where it needed to start.

When I returned to America, I shared with the women and their church the whole chain of events and how their simple acts of kindness set this all in motion. Then I tasked them to pray that the innocent prisoners would be completely set free, because I had heard they were still in jail one month later. I also tasked them to pray for the entire judicial system of Benin.

In my speaking engagements throughout the USA, these innocent prisoners became a big prayer point for various church groups that wanted to be involved. To my great surprise, just one month after the church prayer groups began to pray, three of the four women were set free. The following month, I got a call from my friend who runs the Orphanage Safe Home in Benin, and she gave me some incredible news. The President of Benin had visited a prison that week. She shared that never in the history of Benin had the President of the country ever visited a prison.

He was appalled by what he saw and heard. He immediately mandated his government cabinet members to work on revamping the entire judicial and prison system. The US State Department was asked to help the Benin government with this process.

My friend in Benin commented to me that they had been praying for years for this to happen, but it wasn't until our friends in the USA started to pray, that there began to be any real action. She said, "Rebecca, whoever you have praying, please tell them to keep it up. God is moving."

One year later, I sat down with the social worker from the prison, and he said that every case in the prison was mandated to be reevaluated during this revamping process. The judges had already set free over twenty percent of the innocent people and many more were going to be released soon.

The fourth woman we had pleaded for was finally released that year. By 2017, over thirty percent of the prisoners in the prisons were released and more cases were being brought to justice. The US State Department allotted funds to build more court houses to accommodate all the cases. New prison facilities were also built that were more accommodating and offered better living conditions. We saw miraculous justice for many prisoners.

There is a different president now and we are not seeing further movement to help innocent prisoners get out of prison. But, what we do know is that God can do this again. So, let's ramp up our prayers again for the many prisoners who need someone to fight for them.

Each time I return to Benin I visit this same judge. Our friendship has grown throughout the years. He has become a great advocate for what Orphan Relief and Rescue is doing in his country. He is the same judge that would tell me of the many children that he was rescuing from becoming trafficked at the borders of Nigeria and is the same judge that challenged us to get into these trafficking villages to see how we could help more children that you just read about in chapter five.

In looking back at these experiences, it is amazing that through simple acts of kindness and the fervent prayers of women from a church on Whidbey Island, Washington, and of many others, a whole chain of events was set into motion: hundreds of innocent prisoners were set free, an entire judicial system in Benin was revamped, children were rescued from being trafficked, not to mention the transformation of entire villages all because God's people were willing to stand in the gap and pray.

Who would have ever guessed what God was planning in the heavenlies to make His kingdom come and His will to be done on earth as it is in heaven through prayer? Amazing!

We each have a part to play. God is inviting us to be a part of carrying out His mission. Without one of the following elements, these changes could not have been accomplished:

- Without ladies sewing dresses for the little girls in Africa, this would not have happened.
- Without churches and prayer groups taking on the challenge to pray, this would not have happened.
- Without people giving money to pay for children to go to school and to eat two meals every day, this would not have happened.
- Without my jumping on a plane to Africa, this would not have happened.
- Without the local nationals, such as the judge being willing to hear my heart for justice, and to partner

with us to rescue children from being trafficked in his country, this would not have happened.

We all work together towards one goal, and it takes all of us to accomplish the full picture of what God wants to do through our lives to set people free. **Everyday God is asking us to pray for His kingdom to come and for His will to be done, here on earth as it is in Heaven.** (Matthew 6:10)

Through Christ we carry more power on earth than we can ever imagine. God handed us the keys to this power through our relationship with Him.

Sometimes we wonder if our prayers really do anything. Are they making an impact? Are people's destinies changed? Are accidents thwarted? Are lives saved? Are nations and people impacted?

In walking through the situation with the judicial system and because of my many other experiences, I can tell you my answer is a big YES! Our prayers can and do make all the difference. Prayer can change lives and circumstances.

We are also reminded of the many people in the Bible who walked out their faith and prayer life and lived to see their prayers answered in often radical ways. There are countless heroes of the faith in the Bible, such as Moses, Joshua, Esther, Daniel, Elijah and many more. Our prayers do affect change, wherever we go and in whatever we do.

*In the Message it says:... **ask the God of our Master, Jesus Christ, the God of glory – to make you intelligent and discerning in*** *knowing him personally, your eyes focused and clear, so that you can see exactly what it is he is calling you to do, grasp the immensity of this glorious way of life he has for his followers, oh, the utter extravagance of his work in us who trust him – endless energy, boundless strength! Ephesians 1:18-19*

Praying with Expectation

It had been three years since we started our Microfinance Program. Mainly women attended these meetings, and many had come to Jesus over those years and had renounced their Voodoo and witchcraft practices.

Each time we were going to reach out to the men, the women on our program requested that we not. They explained that if their husbands knew they were hearing about Jesus and choosing to follow Him, they would be forbidden to come to these meetings.

In light of the women's concerns, we were extra cautious about our meetings with them. Yet three years later, we felt a sense of peace about reaching out to the men.

We had a team from the USA with us in Benin. This team had a great group of men, and we felt confident they could host the first official men's meeting in Benin. My husband Tim would lead them into the village with our Beninese anti-trafficking team of local employees.

After breakfast, we women on the USA team gathered around the men and prayed for them before they left for the village. We asked God to bring men of influence to the men's meeting, and that these men would accept Jesus into their lives.

Upon the return of our two teams, we eagerly antici-
pated hearing the details. The men began to share the
beautiful things that God had done. The chief of the village and his village elders, along with a large group of
men from the community, had shown up to participate.

The team members shared their personal testimonies
and then our Western pastor, along with our Benin pastor,
gave an altar call for those who wanted to receive Jesus into
their lives. To their great surprise, the chief of the village,
his elders, and many other men from the community, came
forward to accept Jesus.

As they shared these details, I was surprised it went exactly as we had prayed. I turned to our anti-trafficking staff
and said, "Wow, this is incredible. Isn't this exciting?"

Our anti-trafficking team was happy but did not seem
to express as much outward enthusiasm as I was displaying.

I then asked our anti-trafficking staff, why they all did
not seem as shocked as we were about all of this? "Please tell
me what is going on in your thoughts right now?" I asked.

**"Oh, Rebecca this is very exciting for sure, but we are
not surprised by this," said one of our local staff. "We
prayed for this to happen, and God answered our prayers.
It is simply what God is doing every day here. We pray and
God answers. You come and go, so you are surprised by
what you are seeing, but we are not. God is moving every
day like this. It is just simply what our God does."**

Their words of faith humbled me. They were right.
Shouldn't this always be our expectation? Shouldn't we
always pray with expectation that God is going to answer?

For me I honestly did not expect God to answer our prayers so quickly or so specifically. I realized my faith, my expectation of what God can do when we pray, was lacking. That day, I was challenged to pray more with expectation for God to show up and to show up big.

If ye abide in me, and my words abide in you, ye shall ask what ye will, and it shall be done unto you. John 15:7 (KJV)

Ask, and it shall be given you; seek, and ye shall find; knock, and it shall be opened unto you: Matthew 7:7 (KJV)

Questions for personal reflection:

- What is something you know you need to commit to pray for more consistently?
- What kind of reminder each day can you give yourself to pray for that certain thing?

Prayer:

Heavenly Father, I thank you for all the answered prayers you have fulfilled in my lifetime. I thank you for being concerned about every detail of my life and for the lives in front of me. I ask that you help me to be more faithful in my prayer times with you. Help me to trust you more and to pray with expectation that you are going to show up. Surprise me around every corner with your faithfulness. In Jesus' name I pray, Amen.

Song: "Way Maker," by Bethel Music

CHAPTER 12

EXTRAORDINARY LIVING THROUGH HEARING GOD'S VOICE

"My sheep hear my voice, and I know them, and they follow me. I give them eternal life, and they will never perish, and no one will snatch them out of my hand."

— John 10:27-28 (ESV)

I am regularly asked how I know it is God that is speaking or prompting me to do something. How do I know it is not just something that I have thought up myself? Through lots of trial and error, this is my thought process in answer to this question.

God is so in love with us and wants to have an intimate relationship with each of us. He is pursuing and speaking to our minds and actively working to get our attention on a daily basis. His desire is to guide and lead us through every circumstance and phase of our lives. He created each of us and knows us better than anyone. He knows what will make us come alive and what will destroy us.

The big question is always can we really recognize God's voice/promptings? The answer is yes. God has given us many avenues to hear Him speak to us. Just as we have learned to recognize our best friend's voice on the phone, we can also learn to recognize God's voice as He uses different ways to speak to us.

Common ways God can speak to us

God speaks through the Bible:

The most powerful tool He has given us is His word, the Bible. The Bible gives us a road map for living a healthy life as God intended for us. If we will live according to God's principles, we will obtain wisdom and discernment and become acquainted with a loving, merciful, powerful and just God.

The character of God is shown strongly all throughout the Bible, as we see a love story revealed. Throughout history He has always been in constant pursuit to redeem, rescue and restore humanity.

As we read, God speaks to the depths of our hearts if we will allow the Holy Spirit to penetrate our minds through His word.

For the word of God is living and active, sharper than any two-edged sword, piercing to the division of soul and of spirit, of joints and of marrow, and discerning the thoughts and intentions of the heart. Hebrews 4:12 (ESV)

Do not merely listen to the word, and so deceive yourselves. Do what it says. James 1:22 (NIV)

God speaks through His creation:

God made the beauty of the earth for us to see His glory all around us so that we would never doubt His existence. As we look at brilliant sunsets, the beautiful sky above, the depth of an ocean, the birth of a newborn baby, God is reminding us that He created all of this for us. These wonders are daily reminders of Himself. He wants us to know that He will never leave us or forsake us.

As we look into the beauty of these things, God is speaking to our souls of His love for us.

The works of the Lord are great, studied by all who have pleasure in them. His work is honorable and glorious, And His righteousness endures forever. He has made His wonderful works to be remembered; The Lord is gracious and full of compassion. Psalms 111:2-4 (NKJV)

For since the creation of the world His invisible attributes are clearly seen, being understood by the things that are made, even His eternal power and Godhead, so that they are without excuse... Romans 1:20 (NKJV)

God speaks through people:

All through the Bible we see how God uses various people as messengers or guides to influence others for good.

The story of Jonah and the whale is a classic biblical example. God sent Jonah to Nineveh to tell the people to repent or face destruction. Jonah was a person delivering a direct message from God.

In listening to people who have a message or counsel that we feel may be from God, we have to be very careful. It can be a wonderful thing when we have godly people surrounding us who have wisdom. God can use these wise people to speak into our hearts as a direct message from God. On the other hand, the negative can happen when someone is not a good representative of Christ in our life. The enemy can be at work to derail us from what God wants to do in our lives. We have to test whether the counsel of those around us conforms to God's word. We can measure whether it seems right and aligns with Scripture through feeling a deep internal sense of peace.

God speaks through a still small voice:

We are reminded in 1 Kings that God also speaks to us through a whisper, as he did with Elijah. If we are not taking time to be alone with God, we will not be able to hear Him whisper which way we should go next.

The Lord said, "Go out and stand on the mountain in the presence of the Lord, for the Lord is about to pass by."

Then a great and powerful wind tore the mountains apart and shattered the rocks before the Lord, but the Lord was not in the wind.

After the wind there was an earthquake, but the Lord was not in the earthquake. After the earthquake came a fire, but the Lord was not in the fire.

*And after the fire **came a gentle whisper**. When Elijah heard it, he pulled his cloak over his face and went out and stood at the* *mouth of the cave. Then a voice said to him, "What are you doing here, Elijah?"... 1 Kings 12:11-13 (NKJV)*

We tend to look for God to speak to us through all our distractions in life, yet God is just wanting us to come away to a quiet place so he can whisper in our ear.

For me this is not an audible voice; it is a strong impression or thought that comes to my mind with a deep sense that it is from the Lord. (I will explain more about this in a moment.)

Are you willing to take that time alone, so you can hear or sense what He is wanting to say to you?

Be still, and know that I am God. Psalms 46:10 (NKJV)

You will seek me and find me when you seek me with all your heart. Jeremiah 29:13 (NIV)

God speaks through music:

We know that when we listen to music sensory areas in our brain are stimulated. When we hear a sad song, we may go into a melancholy and somber state of mind. If we hear a happy song, our spirits seem lifted up and we instantly feel hopeful and encouraged. If we hear a worshipful song, we can feel connected to God in a fresh new way.

We look at how King Saul in the Bible used music to improve his state of mind when he was feeling down. In these times he would have David, who would later become king, play the harp for him. The music was the only thing that would soothe his spirit.

Once David became king, he was known for his love for music. The psalms are full of the songs he wrote pouring his heart out to God. It was clear that he felt the closest to God when he was worshipping.

I find that when I listen to worship music, I am able to shut out the problems of my day and can fully focus on the one who created me. A fresh intimacy with God comes during these times, and it sets the stage for my mind to be more receptive to hear what God is trying to say to me. God has brought incredible clarity in times of distress, hopelessness, and confusion, through listening to worship music.

Some of the songs I have put at the end of the chapters in this book have been ones that God has used to speak to my heart with regards to important matters in my life.

As our walk with God grows and we begin to identify God's voice more clearly, God reveals more of His heart to us. We begin to see His character in ways we never saw before. We are able to embrace His love for us and for all of humanity. We are able to see His heart's desire to bring restoration to our lives and the lives of those near us.

As we start recognizing His voice, He begins to ask us to do things, such as pray for someone; give a word of encouragement to someone; give of our resources or time. We then have full and complete free will to either do that certain thing or not. The choice is ours. What I have learned, is that if we will do what He asks of us, we will come alive in a way we have never experienced before, being fulfilled in ways we had never dreamed could happen. Through obedience we begin to understand what we were actually created to be and to do on this earth, which gives us a sense of freedom and peace. A beautiful partnership and intimacy with Christ forms. It is exciting to see others walk in this freedom and intimacy with Christ as well. We then will automatically want to share this extraordinary life with others.

...Does the Lord delight in burnt offerings... as much as in obeying the voice of the Lord? To obey is better than sacrifice... 1 Samuel 15:22 (NIV)

How can I tell the difference between God's voice, the enemy's voice, and my own voice? Here are some ways that I determine if it is God's Spirit speaking to me about something He is wanting me to do.

Ways to determine if it is God speaking:

1. **Did God disrupt my daily routine or sleep to get my attention about this situation and the feeling/ thought won't go away?**
2. **Is this request/prompting from God out of my comfort zone?** If yes, then it very likely is God. Rarely has something God asked me to do been comfortable.
3. **Is it something I would have not normally thought of myself?** This is another indication it is probably from God. He puts these thoughts in our mind.
4. **Does it have to do with, redeeming, rescuing and/ or restoring your life or someone else's life?** That is the business God is always in. It could be as simple as

praying for healing for someone, doing something for someone you normally would not think of doing, or granting forgiveness to someone.

5. **Does it align with God's heart and what He asks us to do in the Bible?**

If I can say yes to ALL these questions, it is a pretty sure thing that it is of God. Then I have a choice. Am I going to act upon what God is asking/prompting me to do or not?

As I choose to obey God, I am then able to see God do some neat and extraordinary things through life, as you have read about here. This type of living is what God wants for each of us.

Ways to determine if the enemy is speaking:

1. **Inner peace will not be there. Your spirit will be agitated and not settled.**
2. **It will not align with what the Bible would say. It goes against the character of God.**
3. **If the activity will be destructive to yourself or those around you, then it is the enemy.**
4. **If you feel you have to do the activity to feel better about yourself, this may be the enemy trapping you into doing something for selfish reasons that will not have God's blessing on it.**
5. **If you are feeling condemned and belittled as a person, that is the enemy.** Condemnation is not the same as feeling convicted. If you are convicted about

something you need to make restitution for, that is God, but if you are feeling condemned for who you are, that is the enemy.

Therefore, there is now no condemnation for those who are in Christ Jesus, ... Romans 8:1 (NIV)

Be alert and of sober mind. Your enemy the devil prowls around like a roaring lion looking for someone to devour. 1 Peter 5:8 (NIV)

The enemy loves to lie to us and tell us how horrible we are as a person, a friend, a mother, or a father. He accuses us of what a failure we are in every area of our life. Satan is full of condemnation. This is not how our God operates.

Or what man is there among you who, if his son asks for bread, will give him a stone? Or if he asks for a fish, will he give him a serpent? If you then, being evil, know how to give good gifts to your children, how much more will your Father who is in heaven give good things to those who ask Him! Matthew 7:9 11 (NKJV)

With our own children, grandchildren, nieces or nephews, do we tell them what a horrible person they are? No, quite the opposite. We tell them how much we love them and what they mean to us. In the same way our Father in Heaven is a good and wonderful God who is always trying to get our attention to show us how much He loves us and how important we are to Him.

It is important that we learn how to receive God's love and affirmation. If we can understand how He feels about us, there is nothing that will stop us from wanting to serve Him.

Here is a practical exercise I like to give people to help them learn how to hear God speak to them. You can do this too, every day if you like.
Sometime today take ten minutes to be alone. Take a piece of paper with you and write down this question: **God, how do you feel about me?** Quiet your heart and mind; maybe look out a window at God's creation. After a couple minutes of quieting your mind, ask God that question. **Then write down the first impression/thought** that comes to your mind.

In doing this exercise, I have learned a few things that tend to happen when trying to hear what God is saying to me and I will share them with you.

The first thought/impression is usually God speaking, the second thought/impression is usually me disputing that it was God speaking to me, and the third thought/impression is usually the enemy telling me that it for sure is not God.

God is usually very quick to respond to our question because He loves to tell us how much He loves us and what He thinks of us. We are the ones who have a hard time receiving it, and the enemy for sure does not want you to accept anything good that God has to say about you.

If your response was negative and it does not align with God's character, then do not accept it. It is not of God. Take some time later and try again. Always remember the character of God that we learn about in Scripture. He is kind, He is loving, He is a good Father, and He is trustworthy.

Question for personal reflection:

- What do you think you heard God say about what He feels about you? Remember you can try this anytime, anywhere to get familiar with God speaking to you.

Prayer:
Heavenly Father, I thank you that you are always trying to get my attention to show me how much you love me, and to tell me what you think of me. Help me to become a better listener of your still small voice. Help me to recognize you more and more every day. In Jesus' name I pray, Amen.

Song: "May God Be Everywhere I Go," Glory & Wonder, by Mosaic MSC

CHAPTER 13

~~~~~~~~~~~~~~~~~~~~~~~~~~~~~

EXTRAORDINARY LIVING THROUGH OUR THOUGHTS AND WORDS

~~~~~~~~~~~~~~~~~~

"Death and life are in the power of the tongue."
– Proverbs 18:21a (NKJV)

"I was locked in a room all day with no food and was very hungry and scared," said Emma, the adorable six-year old girl standing in front of me. With all the passion she could muster, she described her life in the village before coming to live in our Orphanage Safe Home in Benin.

In meeting this bright-eyed beautiful girl for the first time, it was hard to believe she had endured such hardship. She had come to our home six months prior.

I introduced myself to her and asked, "Emma, do you like living here in your new big house?"

"Oh, yes, I love living here," she quickly responded.

"Why do you love living here?" I continued.

"Because no one beats me and I have plenty of food to eat each day," she replied.

"Emma, can you tell me how your life was in the village and who beat you?" I asked.

"The woman I lived with would beat me every day, over and over for no reason. The man would lock me in a room all day with no food when he would go to work in the fields. I was always hungry," she said. She proceeded to tell me that now she is so happy because she does not have to be hurt by them any longer.

I reached my arms out to Emma and asked if I could hug her. "Oh, yes!" she said, and immediately came close so I could embrace her in a big hug.

"Emma, I am so sorry you were beaten and not fed well by those who were supposed to protect and care for you. We love you, and God loves you so much, and we will always work hard to make sure you are safe from now on," I told her.

"Thank you," she said, with her beautiful bright smile. She then went on her way to play with the other children. She seemed not to have a care in the world.

But it was not always this way. When she first came to our home, she was a very wounded little girl – emotionally, physically and spiritually. Our staff had to work extensively with her. They introduced her to our amazing God of love, who has a wonderful plan for our lives. They told her how valuable and important she is. These were things she had never heard before.

Words of life and healing were regularly prayed over her.

I often am asked if the children we help are ever totally healed in their minds after such abuse. I can honestly answer a strong yes. I have watched children who have been abused in unimaginable ways, have their minds fully restored. Being restored does not mean condoning what has happened but rather, overcoming any malice or resentment toward the abuser.

We learned in the early years of our work with abused children the importance of speaking and praying life over each one. We also realized that helping victims forgive those who have harmed them is key to their being set free to love others.

We have watched transformation after transformation happen in their hearts as they walk in a deep level of gratefulness for their new life. They rarely talk of their past; they focus fully on their future.

I have learned a lot from them about choosing to be thankful for the little things, even when they have been dealt an unfair hand in life. I have seen first-hand how **a thankful heart defeats despair. It is difficult to go into despair when we have a thankful heart.**

For as he thinketh in his heart, so is he. Proverbs 23:7 (KJV)

In my own life, I could not do what I do and see what I see, without walking through life with a grateful heart. I see so much neglect, abuse and all-around mistreatment of human life, particularly with children. **I can allow my mind to go deep into despair with what I see, or I can focus on all that I *do* see God doing.**

Do not conform to the pattern of this world, but be transformed by the renewing of your mind. Then you will be able to test and approve what God's will is – his good, pleasing and perfect will. Romans 12:2 (NIV)

We see throughout the Bible how important it is to have a grateful heart and to focus on loving and forgiving others on a regular basis. Now through science and technology it is possible to see into the brain. Scientists are now catching up to what Jesus and the biblical scholars have been teaching us for thousands of years. Our thinking and our words really do change our brains, not in some magical way, but in a real physical way.

The science is called neuroplasticity. It means that our thoughts can change the structure and function of our brains. Through neuroplasticity scientists are proving the brain is endlessly adaptable and dynamic. It has the power to change its own structure, even for those with severe neurological afflictions. **This means that with repetitive positive thought and positive activity, it is possible to rewire the brain and strengthen those areas that stimulate positive feelings.**

In his widely acclaimed book, *The Brain that Changes Itself,* Norman Doidge, M.D., talks about how "the brain has the capacity to rewire itself and/or form new neural pathways."

He talks about the importance of doing the work, "just like exercise, [which] requires repetition and activity to reinforce new learning."[2]

Some health benefits of positive thinking include:

- Increased life span
- Lower rates of depression
- Better psychological and physical well-being

Other important factors affecting a healthy brain actually include learning to forgive others and choosing to have a heart of gratitude. **"The practice of forgiveness has been linked to having better immune function and a longer lifespan**, Other studies have shown that forgiveness has more than just a metaphorical effect on the heart; it can actually lower our blood pressure and improve cardiovascular health as well."[3]

Giving thanks for the good aspects of life also has a powerful impact on our health.

In the article "How Do Thoughts and Emotions Affect Health," the author refers to the work of Brené Brown who "discusses the relationship between joy and gratitude. Acknowledging the good aspects of life and giving thanks have a powerful impact on emotional wellbeing. In a landmark study, people who were asked to count their blessings felt happier, exercised more, had fewer physical complaints, and slept better than those who created lists of hassles.

Brené Brown has found that there is a relationship between joy and gratitude, but with a surprising twist. **It's not joy that makes us grateful, but gratitude that makes us joyful.**"[4]

Negativity, on the other hand, has a damaging effect. "Chronic stress from negative attitudes and feelings of helplessness and hopelessness can upset the body's hormone balance and deplete the brain chemicals required for feelings of happiness, as well as have a damaging impact on the immune system."[5]

According to Andrew Newberg, M.D., and Mark Robert Waldman, **words can also literally change your brain.** In their book *Words Can Change Your Brain*, they write, "a single word has the power to influence the expression of genes that regulate physical and emotional stress."[6]

According to the authors, **"positive words, such as 'peace' and 'love' can alter the expression of genes, strengthening areas in our frontal lobes and promoting the brain's cognitive functioning. They propel the motivational centers of the brain into action, according to the authors, and build resiliency.**

Conversely, hostile language can disrupt specific genes that play a key part in the production of neurochemicals that protect us from stress. Humans are hardwired to worry – part of our primal brains protecting us from threats to our survival – so our thoughts naturally go there first."[7]

The authors contend that **using the right words can transform our reality:** "By holding a positive and optimistic [word] in your mind, you stimulate frontal lobe activity. This area includes specific language centers that connect directly to the motor cortex responsible for moving you into action. And as our research has shown, the longer you concentrate on positive words, the more you begin to affect other areas of the brain. Functions in the parietal lobe start to change, which changes your perception of yourself and the people you interact with. **A positive view of yourself will bias you toward seeing the good in others, whereas a negative self-image will lead you toward suspicion and doubt. Over time the structure of your thalamus will also change in response to your conscious words, thoughts, and feelings, and we believe that the thalamic changes affect the way in which you perceive reality."**[8]

How we choose to live our life and what we choose to think about are choices that really do affect our health and wellbeing.

And let the peace of Christ rule in your hearts, to which indeed you were called in one body. And be thankful. Let the word of Christ dwell in you richly, teaching and admonishing one another in all wisdom, singing psalms and hymns and spiritual songs, with thankfulness in your hearts to God. And whatever you do, in word or deed, do everything in the name of the Lord Jesus, giving thanks to God the Father through him. Colossians 3:15-17 (ESV)

Keeping in mind what scientists have learned about the brain, think about the implications for a person's spirit. When we extend words of kindness and encouragement to someone, we are literally breathing words of life into someone's spirit. When we spit angry and bitter words at someone, we are spewing death upon their hearts and minds.

The spiritual dynamics in play with our mouths activate the spirit world to take action, whether to bless or to curse. The Bible talks about this power in James 3:3-5 (NIV): *When we put bits into the mouths of horses to make them obey us, we can turn the whole animal. Or take ships as an example. Although they are so large and are driven by strong winds, they are steered by a very small rudder wherever the pilot wants to go. Likewise, the tongue is a small part of the body, but it makes great boasts.*

In Benin, where witchcraft and sorcery are intertwined in every aspect of life, people are very aware of what words can do. When people in this region, who are not followers of Jesus, do not like what someone is doing or feel threatened by someone, they literally speak curses over them. They pray to their gods to put spells on people, and the dark spirit world causes havoc in people's lives through these curses.

On the other hand, people who are followers of Jesus, know that the power of their prayers can dispel any curse of harm or sickness. Praying blessing, healing, and freedom upon someone's life activates God's spirit to sweep through his/her life. We do not fully know how God does this, but this does happen in the spirit world that we cannot see. I can guarantee you, I have witnessed this in very powerful and phenomenal ways.

All through the Scriptures Jesus is asking us to ask for what we need. When we ask according to God's perfect will, to **redeem, rescue or restore,** He will answer in a way He knows best. God is trustworthy in this.

Until now you have not asked for anything in my name. Ask and you will receive, and your joy will be complete. John 16:24 (NIV)

If you ask Me anything in My name, I will do it. John 14:14 (ESV)

If we truly knew the power that we carry through our words, we would live and speak differently. Imagine the freedom and healing that would be possible if we declared many more blessings over our lives and the lives of those around us.

Consider the life of Ezekiel. In Ezekiel 37 (ESV), I love how God showed him, through a vision, how the power of prophesying (declaring), over our lives can bring life to our bodies, minds, and spirits.

The hand of the Lord was upon me, and he brought me out in the Spirit of the Lord and set me down in the middle of the valley; it was full of bones. And he led me around among them, and behold, there were very many on the surface of the valley, and behold, they were very dry. And he said to me, "Son of man, can these bones live?" And I answered, "O Lord God, you know." Then he said to me, "Prophesy over these bones, and say to them, O dry bones, hear the word of the Lord. Thus says the Lord God to these bones: Behold, I will cause breath to enter you, and you shall live. And I will lay sinews upon you, and will cause flesh to come upon you, and cover you with skin, and put breath in you, and you shall live, and you shall know that I am the Lord."

So I prophesied as I was commanded. And as I prophesied, there was a sound, and behold, a rattling, and the bones came together, bone to its bone. And I looked, and behold, there were sinews on them, and flesh had come upon them, and skin had covered them. But there was no breath in them. Then he said to me, "Prophesy to the breath; prophesy, son of man, and say to the breath, Thus says the Lord God: Come from the four winds, O breath, and breathe on these slain, that they may live." So, I prophesied as he commanded me, and the breath came into them, and they lived and stood on their feet, an exceedingly great army.

Then he said to me, "Son of man, these bones are the whole house of Israel. Behold, they say, 'Our bones are dried up, and our hope is lost; we are indeed cut off.' Therefore prophesy, and say to them, 'Thus says the Lord God: Behold, I will open your graves and raise you from your graves, O my people. And I will bring you into the land of Israel. And you shall know that I am the Lord, when I open your graves, and raise you from your graves, O my people. And I will put my Spirit within you, and you shall live, and I will place you in your own land. Then you shall know that I am the Lord; I have spoken, and I will do it, declares the Lord."

Let's begin to declare over our own personal dry bones that they come alive. Our dry bones could be our failing health, our failing marriages, our failing finances, or all-around discouraging circumstances. Whatever hard place we may find ourselves in that need a touch from Jesus, let's declare what we need from the Lord. Today let's speak life over our souls and the lives of those in our path. **Let's have this year be the year of declaration for all that we need God to help us with.**

Stop listening to the lies of the enemy and stand on the promises that God gives us as His children. Spend time with Him so you can get a right perspective of how much He loves you. He is our greatest protector and comforter in every circumstance.

Questions for personal reflection:

- What do I need to declare victory for in my life?
- What lies have I been listening to that I need to silence?

Prayer:
I declare health over my body, mind, and spirit. I declare blessing, health, protection, favor, direction, wisdom, and provision over my life and over the lives of my family and friends' lives, and my business dealings. I declare wisdom and protection for our country and state leaders and our church leaders. I declare unselfish and honest motives for the leaders in every country, and that your Holy Spirit

would touch the heart of each one of them. In Jesus' name I pray, Amen.

You can speak and declare blessing over your life from Psalms 103 (I changed the word your, to my)

> *Bless the Lord, O my soul,*
> *and all that is within me,*
> *bless his holy name!*
> *Bless the Lord, O my soul,*
> *and forget not all his benefits,*
> *who forgives all my iniquity,*
> *who heals all my diseases,*
> *who redeems my life from the pit,*
> *who crowns me with steadfast love and mercy,*
> *who satisfies me with good*
> *so that my youth is renewed like the eagle's.*

Song: "The Blessing," by Elevation Worship with Kari Jobe and Cody Carnes

CONCLUSION

~~~~~~~~~~~~~~~~~~~~~~~~~~~~~~~~~~~~

CHAPTER 14

THE ULTIMATE KEY TO LIVING AN EXTRAORDINARY LIFE

~~~~~~~~~~~~~~~~~~~~~~~~~~~~~~~~~~~~

"If you cling to your life, you will lose it; but if you give up your life for me, you will find it."

— Matthew 10:39 (NLT)

I recently watched a movie *The Couple*, a true story about an extremely wealthy Jewish man and his family caught in the Nazi persecution in the 1940's in Germany. He was given two choices. The first choice was to sign over his entire fortune of homes, businesses and assets to the Nazi government in exchange for his family's life. The second choice was to keep everything and to watch all his loved ones die before his eyes.

This movie showed his immense love for his family and the pain of his sacrifice in giving up all his earthly possessions that he worked a lifetime to accumulate, to ensure his family would be saved. The subtitle read, "His sacrifice was their salvation."

I have learned that anything of value has cost someone somewhere something. Our freedom in America has cost our military and their families much pain and loss. Making sure our children are raised in a healthy manner costs. Keeping our bodies healthy, physically and spiritually, takes discipline and costs us time and money. The work we are doing in Africa is full of sacrifice. Without the sacrifice of many selfless individuals none of these rescue missions could take place.

Nothing is for free. Someone somewhere has had to pay for what comes as freedom to others. This is what Jesus did for us. He paid the highest price on the cross with His life as the ultimate sacrifice for our sins, past, present, and future.

Through Christ's death, He has given us a chance at a life of freedom and eternity with Him when we accept Him into our lives. His ultimate sacrifice brought our ultimate freedom.

My father used to tell me a story of when he felt the call into full time mission work in Mexico. He said it was in a church service on Whidbey Island in Washington, where the special speaker, a man named Danny Ost, was in missions. Listening to this man speak became the beginning of my father's deciding to change the course of his life.

Danny said, "**If our faith isn't costing us something, then it is not worth very much.**" My father said that statement bothered him to the core. He knew he was a comfortable Christian, that his faith really wasn't costing him anything. But now he felt restless with the mundane and knew there was more that God wanted from him.

He was soon off to commit the next seventeen years of his life to missions in Mexico, a decision that would forever alter the course of his life, and the life of his future family. Due to my father's sacrifice to the Lord's calling on his life, each of his five children grew up with a heart for the extraordinary adventurous life in partnership with Christ.

There are kingdom principles outlined in Scripture that illustrate how the degree of our sacrifice is comparable to the level of our spiritual impact. A few biblical examples are Esther, Daniel, Moses, Elijah, and Paul. Their sacrifices had long-lasting spiritual consequences.

There is great blessing associated with participating with God and sacrificing for His kingdom purposes. This does not mean we do not enjoy life and have fun; it means that we are purposefully sacrificing our selfish desires in order to bless others.

There is an emptiness associated with being self-focused. When God asks us to sacrifice resources, time and energy, it is incredibly fulfilling.

When working in Africa rarely do things go as planned. Accomplishing even simple tasks takes more time, money, sweat, and energy than ever expected. Nothing comes easy; this work is not for the faint-hearted. Even the flights to get there are long and uncomfortable. At the same time, God shows up in extraordinary ways over and over again. He actually has to if things are going to even work there. I have also seen that He takes care of us, as we extend our hand to help others. *Whoever gives to the poor will not want... Proverbs 28:27a (ESV)*

Do not neglect to do good and to share what you have, for such sacrifices are pleasing to God. Hebrews 13:16 (ESV)

A huge life altering lesson I have learned in my service to God and others, is that when we listen, and act upon that still small voice that says "walk this way, help this person, or speak kindly to this person," then beautiful things happen all around us, here in America and abroad. **Our action of obedience activates God's perfect will to be accomplished** through our lives. Obedience is not always comfortable, but the results are amazing.

In Matthew 10:39 when Jesus said, **"If you cling to your life, you will lose it; but if you give up your life for me, you will find it."** I have found this to be true on every level. It is the most important thing I have learned in my life. **Our personal death to our selfish desires is the main key to our being able to live an Extraordinary life.** Without this one component, we can do and say what seems right, yet it will not reach the Extraordinary. **Extraordinary living can only happen when we choose daily to give up our life for the sake of what God is asking of us.** When I give up my will, my comfort, time, sleep, finances when God asks, for the sake of those in need around me, I find out who I truly am, and what I was created to do in partnership with the greatest lover of all of humanity.

I love how the author James Finley described this truth: **Our deepest freedom rests not in our freedom to do what we want to do but rather in our freedom to become who God wills us to be.**[9]

I have found that there is no greater life than this. We get the privilege to live an Extraordinary life when we choose daily to serve and to hand our life over to our Extraordinary God!

Question for personal reflection:

- What are you clinging to that you know God wants you to give up, to sacrifice at His feet?

Prayer:
Heavenly Father, thank you for creating me and for loving me so wholeheartedly every day of my life. Thank you for making the ultimate sacrifice on the cross for my sins, so that I can live free. I never want to take for granted what you have done for me. Please help me to daily give up my selfish desires so that you can shine through my life. Help me not to live for myself, but to live full heartedly for you. In Jesus' name I pray, Amen.

Song: "At the Cross," by Chris Tomlin (Passion 2014)

ABOUT REBECCA

Rebecca has been involved in Christian humanitarian work for twenty years. Rebecca, her husband Tim, and their friends Matt Le Page and Don Clark, co-founded Orphan Relief and Rescue in 2007.

Rebecca and Tim live in the USA. Rebecca works full time as the President of Orphan Relief and Rescue, and her husband works full time in his painting, landscape and design business. They have three married children and seven biological grandchildren. They also have hundreds of "children of the heart" in Africa.

Rebecca is passionate about inspiring people to take action on behalf of the poor and needy around the world and is equally passionate about challenging and inspiring people to walk closely with God, and to trust Him fully with their lives.

Rebecca's first book, *Inspired to Action, How Following the Promptings of Your Heart Can Change the World*, describes the journey of Orphan Relief and Rescue's work in Africa. Through this work God opened her eyes to how amazing and big He is, as she stepped out in faith to work in partnership with Him.

Everything she is sharing in *Inspired to Live an Extraordinary Life* has come from her life's experiences of incredible hardship and overwhelming joy.

ABOUT ORPHAN RELIEF
AND RESCUE

At Orphan Relief and Rescue (ORR) we work to overcome injustice in the areas of abuse, neglect, and trafficking for underserved children in Benin and Liberia, West Africa.

We believe that every child has a name, dream and destiny, and we are working hard to ensure that they are given a voice and hope for the future.

We work with orphaned, abandoned and abused children who have simply been forgotten.

In Benin: ORR has developed programs in the areas of Intervention, Rescue, Restoration and Empowerment, which are administered by our local national staff. These programs are described here.

Intervention: ORR collaborates with local leaders to identify children at high risk of being trafficked and engage intentionally to prevent those children from being sold. Children who are intercepted from trafficking are placed in our Intervention Program, which aims to remove barriers that guardians/parents face in keeping their children home. Through providing food and an education, guardians have little motivation to sell their children.

Rescue: ORR works diligently to identify and bring back children who have been sold into a life of slavery. When possible these children are placed with their families and are re-enrolled in school and placed in our Intervention Program. If this is not possible for the child's safety, then the child is placed in Foster Care or in one of Orphan Relief and Rescue's Safe Homes.

Restoration: Children who have been rescued from slavery and are too old to return or begin school are put into an apprenticeship program such as in electrical, mechanics, sewing/tailoring, or hair dressing. They are also provided two meals a day by ORR.

Empowerment: ORR directly addresses the issues of poverty, providing caregivers with the opportunity to improve their situation through provision of micro-loans, basic business training, and introduction to the savings and loans program. These small loans provide enough to sustain the necessities of life and allow parents to provide for their children and not sell them into slavery.

In Liberia: ORR has created a program called Break the Silence. This program uses a child friendly tool (a flip chart) to teach children about their rights against sexual and physical abuse, and also shares about the dangers of child trafficking. With this flip chart, in partnership with the Liberian government and non-governmental organizations, ORR has currently taught thousands of children to be aware of their personal rights against such abuses. Children are also connected to an anti-trafficking and abuse hotline that ORR funds, should they find themselves vulnerable to trafficking and/or exploitation. This hotline is hosted by the Ministry of Labor's government office and is the only working anti-abuse hotline in the country. The knowledge of this hotline also acts as a deterrent to would be perpetrators.

Greater Opportunity Educational Scholarship Program: We continue to have strong relationships with orphanage directors and children in homes that we originally helped to get up to healthy and sanitary conditions in our early years of ORR, that you can read about in Rebecca's first book called *Inspired to Action*. We are currently helping older children age out of these orphanage homes in a healthy manner through this educational scholarship program.

In both Benin and Liberia we have great relationships with local governments and local communities. We always work alongside the local community to help bring about solutions for each child. We always want to see the local communities helping their own wherever possible. We only intervene into a child's life when we can't find anyone else to ensure that particular child will be safe.

Our desire is to redeem a lost generation of children. We have studied the problems and tested the solutions and we are making an incredible difference with people who are choosing to help us in these efforts.

Here are some ways you can take action and partner with us today:

- **Become a monthly donor or make a one-time gift. You can donate through our website www.orphanreliefandrescue.org, mail a check made out to Orphan Relief and Rescue, or call our office at 206-453-3158.**
- Sponsor a project or an individual child.
- Host a benefit dinner or fundraiser at your home or church.
- Come visit the children in Benin or Liberia.
- Be an advocate and pray for the children.

We cannot keep this dream alive without you.

To have Rebecca speak to your group, visit www.orphanreliefandrescue.org/speaking.

To follow Rebecca personally through her website, go to www.rebeccampratt.com.

ENDNOTES

1 "Trafficking in Persons Report 2009," The US Department of State, (archived content 2009-2017), https://2009-2017.state.gov/j/tip/rls/tiprpt/2009/index.htm, https://2009-2017.state.gov/documents/organization/123357.pdf, (Page 80).

2 Norman Doidge, M.D., *The Brain That Changes Itself: Stories of Personal Triumph from the Frontiers of Brain Science*, https://www.brainmaster.com/software/pubs/brain/contrib/The%20Brain%20That%20Changes%20Itself.pdf, as summarized in Barrie Davenport, "How Positive Thinking Rewires the Brain," Steven Aitchison (blog), https://www.stevenaitchison.co.uk/how-positive-thinking-re-wires-your-brain/.

3 Karen Lawson, M.D., Expert Contributor, "How Do Thoughts and Emotions Affect Health?", Taking Charge of Your Health and Wellbeing, University of Minnesota (website), n.d., https://www.takingcharge.csh.umn.edu/how-do-thoughts-and-emotions-affect-health.

4 Lawson, "How Do Thoughts and Emotions Affect Health."

5 Carol Bradley Bursack, "Negative Thinking Is Risky for Health," January 6, 2016, Health Central, https://

www.healthcentral.com/article/negative-thinking-is-risky-for-health.

6   Andrew Newberg, M.D. and Mark Robert Waldman, *Words Can Change Your Brain,* as quoted in Therese J. Borchard, "Words Can Change Your Brain," PsychCentral, updated May 2019, http://psychcentral.com/blog/archives/2013/11/30/words-can-change-your-brain/.

7   Newberg and Waldman, as summarized in Borchard.

8   Newberg and Waldman, as quoted in Borchard.

9   James Finley, "Freedom: An Infinite Possibility of Growth," Center for Action and Contemplation, June 15, 2020, https://cac.orgd/author/james-finley/.

.